WRITERS' HOUSES

WRITERS' HOUSES

Where Great Books Began

NICK CHANNER

ROBERT HALE • LONDON

ISBN 978-0-7198-0664-3

Robert Hale Limited
Clerkenwell House
Clerkenwell Green
London EC1R 0HT

www.halebooks.com

A catalogue record for this book is available from the British Library

2 4 6 8 10 9 7 5 3 1

Printed in China

CONTENTS

LONDON

CENTRAL SOUTHERN ENGLAND

THE MIDLANDS

AYRSHIRE

THE BORDERS

DUMFRIES & GALLOWAY

WALES

SOUTH WALES

NORTH WALES

WRITERS' RETREATS

FOREWORD

I DOUBT IT WILL come as much of a surprise to learn that, all my life, I have been intrigued by places, almost as much as by people; and, among those places, the English private house has had a considerable influence on my work. Not just the great country houses, which in the past could almost be considered worlds apart, whole universes crammed into an estate sufficient unto themselves; but also smaller houses, farmhouses and rectories and cottages, each with their own distinctive mood and colour, redolent of the lives that have been lived there. It is no exaggeration that when a house plays an important part in a story, as it does in *Downton*, casting the role is as crucial and delicate as choosing the leading actors. Great was our joy and relief when we first realised that Highclere Castle had every quality needed by *Downton Abbey* and plenty more of its own.

In this book, Nick Channer explores the influence of place on creative writers, searching out their homes and exploring the synthesis between their literary creations and the rooms in which they were imagined and written. My special interest among the men and women he has chosen to analyse is Lucy M. Boston, whose *Green Knowe* books figured largely in my childhood and one of them, *The Chimneys of Green Knowe*, would become a favourite of mine among my own work, filmed as *From Time to Time*. Nothing could interest me more than to read how much of the inspiration for these stories came from Ms Boston's ancient, venerable and yet mysterious home, The Manor at Hemingford Grey. I have visited the house since I shot the movie and walked along the river there. And I can only say I agree with every one of Nick Channer's findings.

I hope you enjoy this book as much as I did.

Julian Fellowes

INTRODUCTION

A SURPRISING NUMBER OF Britain's greatest houses have inspired some of our best-loved literature. It would be difficult to imagine *Great Expectations* without Miss Havisham's squalid, rat-infested home, or Evelyn Waugh's *Brideshead Revisited* without the extravagance and grandeur of Lord Marchmain's stately pile.

Some of these houses reflect little-known literary links. For example, an ancient manor house on the banks of the River Ouse near Huntingdon inspired children's author Lucy M. Boston to write the magical *Green Knowe* stories, while an Elizabethan mansion on the Thames might well have fired Kenneth Grahame's imagination when he was seeking a house on the river as the model for Toad Hall.

Even Sir Arthur Conan Doyle's great detective, Sherlock Holmes, has a part to play in the story of Britain's writers and houses. Groombridge Place, known to the author and only a short distance from his Sussex home, is the setting for a classic Holmes mystery, albeit by a different name. The narrator in *The Valley of Fear* is, of course, Dr John Watson, whose description of the garden at Birlstone Manor was inspired by the garden at Groombridge Place:

> I took a stroll in the curious old-world garden which flanked the house. Rows of very ancient yew trees cut into strange designs girded it round. Inside was a beautiful stretch of lawn with an old sundial in the middle, the whole effect so soothing and restful that it was welcome to my somewhat jangled nerves.

Around the country are a great many houses where Britain's leading authors and poets were born, grew up and found inspiration among their surroundings. Many of the houses are open to the public and offer a fascinating insight into the daily routine of those who resided there, illustrating most effectively the living conditions of the day and how these writers applied themselves to their art.

Among them is D.H. Lawrence's birthplace near Nottingham, a modest back-street terraced house that has been transformed into an exceptionally interesting and informative museum reflecting an authentic family home of the late Victorian period.

Just a few miles to the east is Newstead Abbey, a vast concoction of countless rooms and corridors, where its heir, the poet Byron, hosted sumptuous parties on a gigantic scale. Newstead regularly bore witness to manifestations of his exuberant behaviour.

The two houses could not be more different and yet they are united by one common factor. They were where two Englishmen from entirely different backgrounds would spend their formative years prior to becoming celebrated figures in the world of literature – one a working-class novelist who courted controversy, the other a strikingly handsome poet and aristocrat described by his mistress, Lady Caroline Lamb, as 'mad, bad and dangerous to know'.

However, exploring Britain's network of houses with literary connections is not simply a matter of assessing the diversity of those writers who lived in them or were inspired by them; the houses themselves often represent a telling picture of Britain's island history and our distinguished architectural heritage.

Knole, in Kent, is one of the National Trust's largest and oldest houses, bearing the stamp of six centuries of history: 'the most utterly old of English houses', wrote the columnist and former Deputy Chairman of English Heritage, Simon Jenkins. Knole's most famous occupant, the writer Vita Sackville-West, likened the house to an ageing woman who 'has had many lovers and seen many generations come and go.' Sackville-West's loyalty lay with the house, not its owners whom she described as 'a rotten lot, and nearly all stark staring mad'.

Far removed from the image of Knole's sprawling acres and convoluted maze of rooms, at the heart of the Home Counties, is an early twentieth-century redbrick villa that may well have caught Betjeman's eye had it been on the route of his famous *Metroland* journey. Looking as if it might easily belong in Surrey's well-tended commuter belt, Shaw's Corner was the home of George Bernard Shaw, whose literary canon continues to enthral and whose plays are still performed today.

Twenty years younger than Shaw's Corner, but similarly suburban in style and appearance is The Kilns, on the outskirts of Oxford. This was the long-term home of the writer C.S. Lewis, its drab, worn interior reflecting the academic's modest lifestyle and antipathy towards material wealth.

Thomas Carlyle's early eighteenth-century townhouse in Chelsea occupies a district of London that, incredibly, was once considered poor and dirty. It was one of many houses in the area, which Carlyle described as 'at once cheap and excellent'. At the time when the Scottish writer lived in Cheyne Row, the immediate surroundings were very different. The view from the front of the house was through well-established elm trees to open ground.

Not surprisingly, among Britain's oldest literary houses is a shrine to which visitors come from all corners of the world. Shakespeare's birthplace in Stratford is a surviving fragment of his world and the town that is synonymous with his name. Milton's Cottage in the Chilterns is another rare relic from centuries past.

Inevitably, all literary pilgrims eventually end up at Haworth, the modest Yorkshire home of the Brontës, where, with the help of his late wife's sister, Aunt Branwell, Patrick Brontë raised six children, all under the age of eight, encouraging the remarkable talent of his precious offspring.

This book is a guide to Britain's writers and the houses that caught their imagination and shaped their craft, that they would have known in childhood and where they laboured for countless hours to produce some of our finest and most enduring literature. With the exception of Menabilly and Old Thatch, the former homes of Daphne du Maurier and Enid Blyton respectively, all are accessible to the public. Unless otherwise stated, both house and garden are open to visitors.

ACKNOWLEDGEMENTS

I AM INDEBTED TO many people who helped me during the research and writing of this book. The following people are those to whom I owe special thanks: Julian Fellowes who kindly agreed to write the foreword, Janet Allan of the Elizabeth Gaskell Society for her help and encouragement, Diana Boston for showing me her fascinating home – The Manor at Hemingford Grey – Geoff Haden for his hospitality at Cwmdonkin Drive (the birthplace of Dylan Thomas in Swansea) and for permitting me to sleep in the poet's bedroom, and Naomi Jones for arranging for me to visit Yr Ysgwrn, the former home of the poet Ellis Evans.

Working on this book allowed me to meet many fascinating people, learn much about our literary heritage and wear my literary detective hat at regular intervals. It has also left me with many vivid memories – not least among them are wonderful images of my spectacular walk at Polridmouth Bay in Cornwall. This fruitful visit provided a good deal of background about Daphne du Maurier and her former home. Equally as rewarding and memorable was a trip to the wild moorland country of the Pennines, in search of those bleak places that inspired the Brontë sisters. In the company of my oldest friend, Ian Knapp, I walked to Top Withins, the darkening skies heralding a dramatic thunderstorm. Given the connection with *Wuthering Heights*, the weather conditions seemed appropriate.

Writing a book is a big investment, demanding a lot of time and effort. At the sharp end, guiding me through the different stages, were my commissioning editor, Alexander Stilwell, and my non-fiction editor, Lavinia Porter, and to them I express my gratitude and appreciation.

ENGLAND

THE SOUTH-WEST

CLOUDS HILL

OWING IN NO SMALL measure to Peter O'Toole's masterly portrayal of him in David Lean's epic 1962 film *Lawrence of Arabia*, T.E. (Thomas Edward) Lawrence is still remembered and revered as one of the great English soldiers of the twentieth century. It was Lawrence who helped lead the Arab revolt against the Turks in the Middle East during the latter half of the First World War. Even today, he is still seen as glamorous, enigmatic yet charismatic; a heroic figure who would not seem out of place in the pages of fiction.

His experiences behind Turkish lines formed the basis for his enduring classic *Seven Pillars of Wisdom* (1926), acknowledged as a fascinating account of the Arab revolt from Lawrence's own perspective, as well as a revealing memoir. He revised the manuscript while living at Clouds Hill, his tiny bolt-hole in the Dorset countryside, which he once described as 'bleak, angular, small, unstable: very like its owner'.

Lawrence discovered the near-derelict, early nineteenth-century cottage in 1923, reputedly while out walking near Bovington Camp, where he was based, a mile or so to the south. During the previous twelve months, he had gone to great lengths to bury his celebrated past and create a new identity, preferring anonymity to glory. At the beginning of the year Lawrence's application to join the RAF was rejected when it emerged he had used an alias – that of John Hume Ross. The recruiting officer was Captain W.E. Johns who created 'Biggles', the fictional flying ace. However, Johns was ordered by higher authority to accept Lawrence, though the manner of his recruitment inevitably prompted press speculation and he was eventually discharged. Undeterred, Lawrence resurfaced in March at the Army Tank Training Camp at Bovington, this time in the guise of Private Thomas Edward Shaw. He adopted the name legally in 1927.

Far enough removed from civilization, Clouds Hill was the ideal retreat, a perfect alternative to barrack-room life, which did not really suit Lawrence. He did not intend actually living at the cottage: as a serving soldier he was required to sleep at Bovington Camp. However, Clouds Hill was where he could write undisturbed and entertain a wide circle of literary friends, including George Bernard Shaw, E.M. Forster, Robert Graves and Thomas Hardy. Above all, he relished the solitude it offered.

When Lawrence first viewed Clouds Hill, the cottage had been unoccupied for some considerable time and was generally in a poor state of repair. There was also evidence of damp. There was no kitchen and no electricity and the cottage did not even boast a lavatory. Nevertheless, he did not hesitate in signing the lease. He wrote to a friend: 'I'm not wholly resourceless in Bovington: found a

The view from Clouds Hill. 'The cottage is alone in a dip on the moor,' Lawrence wrote in a letter in 1924. 'Very quiet, very lonely, very bare. I don't sleep here, but come at 4.30pm till 9pm nearly every evening, & dream, or write or read by the fire …'

ruined cottage near camp and took it for 2/6 a week. Have roofed it and am flooring it. At present one chair and a table there ... Scruffy place. About a dozen good books already.'

Built to house a farm labourer, the rudimentary, four-room dwelling reflected Lawrence's unconventional character and reclusive nature. He was not in the least materialistic and had little time for domesticity, maintaining that ten minutes per day was enough time to devote to household chores. He wrote: 'While I have it there shall be nothing exquisite or unique in it. Nothing to anchor me.'

Lawrence later bought the freehold and carried out various improvements to the cottage, intending to live there in retirement. He installed a water supply and, when the main room downstairs was dry enough, he added bookshelves for his many volumes. The room is still dominated by a large leather divan, which doubles as a sofa on which visitors sat and Lawrence sometimes sprawled and read.

The room above includes a typewriter and an acoustic gramophone complete with 78 rpm records. Lawrence would entertain friends in this room, listening to music, writing and relaxing. He turned it into a bedroom when his mother lived at Clouds Hill for a year, and his brother spent his honeymoon there. It remained Lawrence's sitting room until the room downstairs was dry enough to use and remedial work complete.

There is also a painting in this room depicting the view from the cottage in the mid-1920s. In Lawrence's time Clouds Hill lay in open heath. Today, the surroundings are more thickly wooded, making the interior quite dark even on a bright day.

The adjoining bunkroom was lined with aluminium foil to help keep it warm and dry. It served as a makeshift kitchen, with tinned food, jams, bread, cheese and fresh food all kept under glass bell jars. Lawrence tended to buy and store food in bulk, with tins of Heinz baked beans a familiar sight. Ten years after Lawrence moved in, he treated himself to his first hot bath at Clouds Hill – on the day the first boiler was installed. By now the cottage was beginning to resemble something vaguely habitable.

Ironically, despite risking life and limb in the field of human conflict, Lawrence died in a routine road accident a short distance from Clouds Hill. On 11 May 1935 he received a letter from the author

Henry Williamson, who, eight years earlier, had published *Tarka the Otter*, a literary classic. In the letter, Williamson requested a meeting with Lawrence on 14 May to discuss an unpublished typescript. As time was short Lawrence decided to send a telegram to confirm the appointment.

On 13 May Lawrence mounted his much-loved Brough motorcycle to make the short journey to Bovington Post Office from where he would send the telegram. During his return to Clouds Hill he collided with two cyclists, unseen in a dip in the road, and was thrown from the motorcycle, receiving serious head injuries. He died in hospital six days later. He was forty-six.

Clouds Hill, today, still largely untouched by the passage of time and now in the care of the National Trust, evokes the memory of this most romantic and paradoxical of characters whose spirit of adventure and bravery resonated with generations of schoolboys and servicemen long after his death. Lawrence's unorthodox but curiously endearing lifestyle sums up a man who always seemed to be the outsider, beyond the boundaries of convention and conformity. The Greek inscription above the front door at Clouds Hill translates roughly as: 'I don't care'. Nor did he.

T.E. Lawrence 1888–1935

Born in Tremadoc, North Wales, Lawrence grew up in Oxford. In the years immediately prior to the First World War, he worked as an archaeologist on the Euphrates where he first encountered the Bedouins. During the Great War, he worked in army intelligence in North Africa. In 1916 he was British liaison officer to the Arab revolt against the Turks and in 1918 he led the British capture of Damascus. Although he did not relish the concept of fame, he had long aspired to be a writer and believed passionately that his exploits as a serving soldier would translate perfectly to the printed page. His account of the Arab revolt became *Seven Pillars of Wisdom*, abridged by himself as *Revolt in the Desert*. The book was a massive success, consolidating Lawrence's reputation as an outstanding soldier. Had he lived, Lawrence would almost certainly have been called upon to play a key role in intelligence and with special forces in the Second World War, his reputation, knowledge and expertise in the field of battle being proven assets.

HARDY'S COTTAGE

IT IS PERHAPS APPROPRIATE that the cottage where Thomas Hardy was born is found deep in the Dorset countryside. Reached on foot along a half-mile stretch of track serving a smattering of other remote dwellings, it lies in the shadow of ancient woodland on the edge of Puddletown Forest. The cottage would be almost impossible to find were it not an important literary shrine. Given its status, signage is surprisingly limited. However, the effort is worth it. The cottage's interior is a faithful recreation Hardy would recognize, its rural, undisturbed setting recalling the writer's early life in this primitive place.

Sparse and modest, the cob and thatch cottage was built by Hardy's great-grandfather, John Hardy, a local man from nearby Puddletown, in 1800 for his son Thomas, a bricklayer. Leaded lights, deep window seats and low ceilings add depth and character to the place, giving it the look of a much older house. The family building business was established here and continued for more than a century. Hardy's grandmother described the cottage as being 'quite alone'.

The son of a stonemason, Thomas Hardy was born in the upstairs middle bedroom at Higher Bockhampton. It was a difficult birth and at first he was believed to be dead. His tiny, frail body was about to be removed from the room when the midwife intervened, shouting: 'Stop a minute: he's alive, sure enough!'

As a boy, Hardy spent much of his time here reading and writing poems about the countryside. In adulthood he moved to London to work as an architect before returning to Dorset to practice locally. After the success of *Far from the Madding Crowd* (1874), he began to write full time.

Hardy died in 1928, though in many respects, perhaps because the vast body of his work dates back to the second half of the nineteenth century, he seems to belong to an earlier age. In his later years he would travel to the cottage by car, often bringing with him friends who were visiting him at Max Gate, his home in Dorchester. He would proudly show them the place of his birth, though he was critical if the cottage appeared shabby or unkempt.

The cottage contains the desk where he wrote *Under the*

Greenwood Tree (1872) and *Far from the Madding Crowd*. Both books were conceived here and draw heavily on the setting. Hardy preferred to write while he was at the scene so that it gave his descriptive prose a sense of freshness and immediacy. It comes as no surprise to find that the uncompromising wasteland of Hardy's Wessex is strongly reflected at Higher Bockhampton, the surrounding landscape steeped in ancient tradition and local folklore. Close by is the Egdon Heath of Hardy's imagination.

Hardy's birthplace lay at the heart of an agricultural community peopled mainly by farm labourers and domestic servants, where the pattern of life would have been familiar and predictable. For many who lived in this rural backwater the harsh, daily routine was a constant, relentless struggle.

The parlour is dominated by a huge Inglenook fireplace, around which visitors and members of the Hardy family would settle, savouring its warmth and enjoying the atmosphere. Young Thomas would sit here, too, listening to their interpretation of local songs and stories.

The small room to the left of the main parlour as one faces the cottage is believed to be where Hardy's father and grandfather worked on their accounts and kept their cash. There are still bars at the window. Worthy of inspection is the bread oven in the kitchen, which lies to the right of the entrance. Constructed of beehive-shaped fire bricks, such is its capacity that up to fourteen loaves could be baked there at a time.

The garden at Higher Bockhampton – as colourful and charming now as it would have been when Hardy played there as a boy – is of the traditional wild flower, cottage variety and stocked with pinks, lavender and marigolds. Adorning the walls are roses, honeysuckle and japonica. Adjoining the garden is an apple orchard. Hardy would take the Bockhampton sweet apples from here and give them to a Dorchester bookseller's son. In return he was permitted to browse in the shop and read the books.

When the Hardy family eventually vacated the cottage, it was returned to the Kingston Maward estate and bought by a local farmer. The first tenant was Hermann Lea, a friend of Hardy's. The National Trust acquired the cottage in 1948.

MAX GATE

MAX GATE WAS THOMAS Hardy's home for more than forty years, from 1885 until his death in 1928. In the summer of 1883, almost ten years after he married Emma Gifford, a solicitor's daughter, Hardy bought a plot of land one mile south-east of Dorchester – the Casterbridge of his novels – and a short walk from the cottage at Higher Bockhampton where he was born. Having drawn up plans of the proposed house, he commissioned his father and brother to build it.

The construction of Max Gate in 1885 encouraged Hardy to take a keen interest in house-building. Though he had trained as an architect, the work was always on behalf of a client or in association with the firm's senior partners. This time he had a completely free rein and the project soon developed into an obsession. Hardy became closely involved in every aspect of the construction and in due course gained a reputation for being over-fastidious. His constant intrusion and interfering in the building of the house resulted in a family dispute and his father vowed never to work for him again.

Hardy acquired the 1½-acre building plot from the Duchy of Cornwall's estate and built the Victorian redbrick villa on the site of a tollgate and an adjacent cottage that was once the home of Mack, the turnpike keeper – hence the name, Max Gate. The overall design of the house could not be described as striking or aesthetically pleasing and the once dark interiors would have added to the sense of gloom. In short, Max Gate was seen as plain and austere.

Hardy chose to build at Dorchester for several reasons. By now he was an established writer, though his greatest work had yet to be produced. The house was a statement of his success and his social standing. He also felt a nagging desire to return to his roots, the remote Wessex landscape of his childhood. Max Gate seemed to fulfil his ambitions perfectly. Surrounded by open land and affording pleasant rural views, the setting was ideal, unlike the situation today, with nearby busy roads and encroaching housing development.

Hardy's commitment to finishing the house, however, masked personal unhappiness. His marriage to Emma lacked warmth and intimacy and as relations between them deteriorated still further, it was to her attic bedroom that Hardy's wife fled. Emma found Max Gate cold and draughty, while he fretted over the cost of building and maintaining it. Within the house the couple lived markedly separate lives.

Against this background of somewhat claustrophobic marital disharmony, Hardy adapted to life at Max Gate and found the place very much to his taste. He made various changes to the house over the years; enlarging it and even moving his study three times. While living at Max Gate, he wrote *Tess of the d'Urbervilles* and *Jude the Obscure* and, within a year of moving in, he had published *The Mayor of Casterbridge*. Hardy also wrote nearly a thousand poems at the house.

Hardy regularly entertained distinguished writers and playwrights at Max Gate. Among those who visited him at his Dorset home were Robert Louis Stevenson, H.G. Wells, Rudyard Kipling and Virginia Woolf. T.E. Lawrence, who spent much of his time at nearby Clouds Hill, was also a friend and visited Hardy while serving incognito at Bovington Camp.

Though Max Gate reflected Hardy's enduring success and his position among the literary élite, the house remained modest in many respects. As was normal in the Victorian era, there was no bathroom and no running water, and maids were obliged to carry jugs up to the bedrooms. Ten years after the house was built, in fact, there was still no bathroom. Hardy and Emma, it seemed, did not embrace the concept of modern conveniences, preferring the water for their basins and hip bath carried up and down stairs by the servants.

Neither gas nor electricity were installed at Max Gate, which was lit by oil lamps. Eventually, in 1920, a bathroom with hot water was added and a telephone was put in on the ground floor, though Hardy, like many of his generation, was wary of the new-fangled contraption and refused to answer it. At the same time the household acquired a wireless set. Emma had died in 1912 and by now Hardy was married to his secretary, Florence Dugdale, who had insisted on certain changes and improvements when she became his second wife in 1914. Hardy, on the other hand, preferred the old routine. He was, by now, eighty years of age and probably too old to change.

By the dawn of the twentieth century Max Gate was a place of literary pilgrimage. Scores of visitors descended on the house, some uninvited. In the afternoon, after several hours' work in his study, Hardy would come downstairs to greet the teatime visitors. The Prince of Wales famously called at Max Gate in 1923. 'My mother,' he reputedly said, 'tells me you have written a book called *Tess of the d'Urbervilles*. I must try it some time.'

Two years before Hardy's death, the author received a visit from Leonard and Virginia Woolf. Reflecting on the occasion in later years, Leonard Woolf recalled: 'The house which he (Hardy) had built for himself at Dorchester, and which, with its sombre growth of trees, seemed to have been created by him as if it were one of his poems translated into brick, furniture and vegetation.'

Max Gate passed to the National Trust in 1948, twenty years after Thomas Hardy's death. More of the house can be viewed today than in previous years though Hardy's study is not on show. Instead, a replica has been created at the Dorset County Museum in Dorchester.

Thomas Hardy 1840–1928

Hardy learnt to play the fiddle as a child. He also developed a deep and abiding love of nature and his surroundings. He was educated in Dorchester and at sixteen years of age he was apprenticed to a Wessex architect. In 1862 he began a five-year term as an assistant architect in London. By the time he returned to Dorset he had already begun his first novel *The Poor Man and the Lady*, which was never published. Many titles followed *Far from the Madding Crowd*, his first published work, including *The Mayor of Casterbridge* (1886), *Tess of the d'Urbervilles* (1891), often described as the most moving and fluently written of Hardy's novels – passionate, bleak and modern for its time – and *Jude the Obscure* (1895).

A writer of exceptional merit, Hardy also became a noted poet, believing poetry to be superior to fiction. His first collection of verse, *Wessex*, was published in 1898. Hardy's books reflect the spirit and essence of the period and capture quite beautifully the mood and atmosphere of the Wessex region. He had an instinctive feel for the landscape and an intimate knowledge of the countryside, giving the settings in his books a strong sense of place.

Thomas Hardy died at Max Gate; his ashes were interred in Westminster Abbey and his heart was buried beneath a yew tree in Stinsford churchyard, a short distance from his birthplace and Max Gate, and close to other members of his family.

GREENWAY

OVERLOOKING A GLORIOUS SWEEP of the River Dart in South Devon, Greenway is one of those wonderfully evocative country house estates that captures the heart the moment one sees it. The Grade II-listed Georgian house has a tangible air of mystery – which isn't really surprising given that Greenway once belonged to Agatha Christie, Britain's best-loved and most successful crime writer. The house even makes an appearance in several of Christie's classic novels.

Hidden down winding West Country lanes, Greenway conveys a sense of exclusivity and romantic isolation. A small ferry boat crosses the Dart between Greenway Quay and the village of Dittisham, and there are regular river cruises from Dartmouth, offering an alternative, greener and more novel means of reaching the 278-acre estate.

It was a boat trip on the Dart more than forty years ago that ignited my interest in Agatha Christie and her work. I was a teenager at the time and on a family holiday in the area. One August

A broad reach of the Dart bordered by lush green hills and luxuriant woods is visible from the Greenway estate, which Agatha Christie described as 'the loveliest place in the world.'

afternoon we took a river cruise upstream towards Totnes. Over the PA system, the captain of the *Western Lady* drew our attention to an imposing white house peeping into view between the trees on the densely wooded east bank of the river. This, apparently, was Greenway, the enchanting holiday retreat of Agatha Christie, the undisputed Queen of Crime.

I recall picturing the author at home that afternoon, gazing out at the boating activity on the river or perhaps strolling in the woodland garden, down towards the boathouse. I found myself instantly drawn to the atmosphere of the place, its unrivalled location and the world she created in her books.

Throughout her life, the novelist and playwright never lost her ties with Devon and the English Riviera. In her autobiography, published posthumously in 1977, Christie describes how, in 1938, she discovered Greenway was on the market: 'One day we saw that a house was up for sale that I had known when I was young, a house that my mother had always said, and I had thought also, was the most perfect of the various properties on the Dart.' In the book, she refers to Greenway as 'the ideal house, a dream house'.

Christie understood Greenway's price to be £16,000, then realized she had misheard the figure. The actual price was £6,000. She bought the house and, with the help of architect and friend, Guilford Bell, restored it to its original late eighteenth-century design.

Previous owners of the house include some of the West Country's most distinguished families – among them the Eltons of Clevedon Court in Somerset and the Bolithos, renowned Cornish bankers. An earlier house on this site was built by Otho Gilbert, whose widow remarried and later bore a son – Walter Raleigh.

Christie sold Greenway to her daughter Rosalind in 1959 but continued to make regular trips to the house until age took its toll. Rosalind and her husband Anthony Hicks remained at Greenway, making it their permanent home. The house was given to the National Trust in 2000 and, following their deaths in 2004 and 2005 respectively, Christie's grandson, Mathew Prichard, generously donated most of its contents.

Following a five-year £5.4 million restoration programme, Greenway opened to the public in 2009. The house today reflects the spirit of Christie and the heyday of the 1950s when, for a few weeks each spring and summer, and over the Christmas period, she and her archaeologist husband Sir Max Mallowan revelled in the delights of this secluded idyll. Greenway is still packed with treasured mementoes and artefacts acquired during Christie's long life, much of which was spent travelling the world.

One of the principal rooms at Greenway is the library, with its striking frieze dating back to the Second World War when the house was requisitioned by the Admiralty and taken over by the United States Navy. Christie describes the frieze in her memoirs:

> In the library, which was their mess-room, an artist (Lt Marshall Lee) had done a fresco round the top of the walls. It depicts all the places where that flotilla went, starting at Key West, Bermuda, Nassau, Morocco and so on, finally ending with a slightly glorified exaggeration of the woods of Greenway and the white house showing through the trees.

The library, with its grand piano, which Christie would often play, was Mathew Prichard's favourite room at Greenway. The library came to life after breakfast every morning as family members and guests came in to read the newspapers. He recalls a deep chair in the corner where his grandmother used to sit and begin her reading for the day, which was voluminous.

Agatha Christie never wrote at Greenway. This was her precious refuge, her escape from the limelight. However, the house was the setting for one fascinating annual tradition that was crucial to the success of her latest novel. Invariably, her books were published in December and, some months ahead of publication, Christie would gather members of the family in the drawing room after dinner to read a chapter from the new novel – described as the 'Christie for Christmas'. Those present were encouraged to unmask the killer. More often than not, Sir Max would suddenly wake from his evening slumber and correctly identify the murderer.

The 'Christie for Christmas' for 1956 was *Dead Man's Folly*, a Hercule Poirot mystery set in the West Country. The Belgian detective arrives at the local railway station where the chauffeur from

Nasse House is waiting for him. The house is clearly modelled on Greenway while the Dart is thinly disguised as the River Helm. 'They went on, down a steep hill through the woods, then through big iron gates and along a drive, winding up finally in front of a big white Georgian house looking out over the river.'

In the story Poirot is invited to present the prizes at a fête being held in the grounds of Nasse House. One of the fête's main attractions is a murder hunt, which, in typical Christie fashion, goes horribly wrong when the body of a girl is found. Not surprisingly, Christie makes Greenway's atmospheric boathouse the key crime scene:

A short steep slope led down to the door of the boathouse, which was built out over the river, with a little wharf and a storage place for boats underneath ... Marlene made no response. She lay quite motionless. The wind blowing gently through the open window rustled a pile of 'comics' spread out on the table. Poirot was frowning. Very gently he pushed Mrs Oliver aside and went and bent over the girl on the floor. A suppressed exclamation came from his lips. He looked up at Mrs Oliver.

'So ... ' he said. 'That which you expected has happened.'

'You don't mean ...' Mrs Oliver's eyes widened in horror. She grasped for one of the basket chairs and sat down. 'You can't mean ... she isn't *dead*?'

Poirot nodded.

'Oh, yes', he said. 'She is dead. Though not very long dead.'

Greenway also appears in *Five Little Pigs* (1943). In the story the artist Amyas Crale dies in the garden of his Devon home, Alderbury, after drinking hemlock-laced beer. Crale's house is based on Greenway. *Ordeal by Innocence* (1958) features Christie's home as Sunny Point House and the nearby town of Dartmouth is thinly disguised as Drymouth.

Agatha Christie's heart lay at Greenway and her spirit still lingers here. With its magical setting and beautiful views over the river, there can be no finer place. The opening of her beloved home to the public allows her many fans a rare glimpse into Christie's fascinating private world.

The River Dart from Greenway's boathouse. In *Dead Man's Folly*, the river becomes the Helm and Greenway is renamed Nasse House. It is clear from Christie's writing that the boathouse inspired the setting for a murder in the story.

Agatha Christie 1890–1976

Born Agatha Mary Clarissa Miller in the Devon resort of Torquay, Christie was the youngest of three children. Her father, Frederick, was an American businessman. During the First World War she worked as a nurse at the town's Red Cross Hospital. When it opened a dispensary, she accepted an offer to work there and completed the examination of the Society of Apothecaries. 'Poisons are neat and clean and really exciting', she wrote. Her time in the dispensary proved useful for other reasons. It gave her knowledge and insight, which she later used to good effect in her role as Britain's leading crime writer.

Christie's first marriage, to Archie Christie, ended in divorce in 1928. Two years later she met and married the distinguished archaeologist Sir Max Mallowan. After Shakespeare and the Bible, she is the most widely read author in the world and her book sales run into billions. In the 1950s three of her plays ran simultaneously on the London stage. *The Mousetrap*, which opened in the West End in 1952, holds the record for being the longest-running stage play in the world. Christie died in frail old age at Wallingford, aged eighty-five.

MENABILLY

IT LOOKS AT FIRST glance like countless other secluded coves carved into Cornwall's magnificently rugged coastline, but Polridmouth (pronounced Pridmouth) Bay is distinctly separate from the rest. Almost certainly better known as a beautifully haunting setting from the pages of a literary masterpiece than yet another dramatic West Country beauty spot, this wonderfully atmospheric place is easily worth the effort of getting there – the last half-mile or so on foot.

The charming sign by the gate at the start of the walk to Polridmouth Bay recalls a slower, more trusting age. It reads: 'This car park is unattended. Please put money (50 pence) in the milk churn by the farmhouse on the way to the beach. Remember, your honesty keeps the price down.'

The path duly passes the milk churn by the farm outbuildings before cutting through a delightful tunnel of trees. Ahead now a blue swathe of the Atlantic edges gloriously into view and in the foreground there are teasing glimpses of the secret, hidden bay that Daphne du Maurier immortalized in her best-selling novel *Rebecca*, published in 1938 and filmed two years later by Alfred Hitchcock. For the book's legions of fans in search of du Maurier's Cornwall, the sense of anticipation as the path approaches the bay is almost overwhelming.

Du Maurier first set eyes on Menabilly, the Georgian house that would eventually become her home, its setting the model for 'secretive and silent' Manderley in the story, when she was an incurable romantic aged just twenty-one. It was while living at nearby Fowey that du Maurier discovered Menabilly, then empty, dilapidated and unloved. In her book *Enchanted Cornwall* (1989) she wrote:

> I would seize every opportunity to explore, to walk for miles ... Soon I discovered with fascination the enchanted woods on the Gribben headland, and one day looking north, inland from the Gribben, I could just make out the grey roof of a house set in its own grounds in the midst of the trees. That would be Menabilly.

The house was shuttered and the drive and garden a tangle of weeds. However, Menabilly possessed du Maurier from the moment she saw it.

Du Maurier was in Menabilly's thrall and under its spell. She knew that one day her dream of living there would come true. In the meantime, its enchanting setting became the inspiration for Manderley, the elusive house of secrets at the core of *Rebecca*, written five years before she acquired the lease. It was in 1943 that she finally moved to Menabilly, restoring the house that would be her family home for the next twenty years.

For centuries the home of the influential Rashleigh family, Menabilly dates back to the reign of Elizabeth I. The original house was destroyed during the English Civil War, leaving only the outer walls. Menabilly was later remodelled and in the 1820s, following a fire, the body of a cavalier was discovered in the cellar. At the time du Maurier signed the lease, the country was at war and the house belonged to Dr Rashleigh, who had spent little time there. The first book she wrote at Menabilly was *The King's General*, published in 1946 and set in the West Country at the time of the English Civil War. In this book she refers to a skeleton being found in the cellar.

Partly influenced by du Maurier's own feelings of jealousy towards a former fiancée of her husband, the core idea for *Rebecca* was inspired by a casual anecdote told to her by the distinguished writer, Sir Arthur Quiller-Couch, who lived in Fowey. It concerned a member of the Rashleigh family who divorced his glamorous wife to marry a much younger woman. The story lingered persistently in du Maurier's mind and gradually she allowed her imagination to shape and craft the sequence of events into a cohesive plot. The result was a dark, gothic novel of extraordinary intensity and atmosphere, demonstrating du Maurier at her best.

In the foreword to *Enchanted Cornwall* du Maurier wrote: 'Places, houses whispered to me their secrets and shared with me their sorrows and joys. And in return I gave them something of myself, a few of my novels passing into the folklore of this ancient place.'

Though Manderley's setting is plainly Cornish, the house is

based on Milton Park, near Peterborough, the ancestral home of the Fitzwilliam family. Du Maurier visited a number of times as a child and remembered its 'mullioned windows, the wide doors open to the library, the great stone hall, the exquisite staircase leading to the minstrel's gallery'.

In the story, Manderley belongs to attractive widower Max de Winter whose first wife, Rebecca, a renowned socialite noted for her beauty and vivacity, was found drowned aboard her sunken yacht, the *Je Reviens*, off the coast near the house. De Winter's new bride, in contrast young and unsophisticated, is the nameless narrator in the book and it is she who finds herself enthralled by Manderley's romantic setting and air of malevolence. But as the shy, insecure second Mrs de Winter she is also intimidated by comparisons to the exquisite Rebecca.

The path around Polridmouth Bay and the view of the Menabilly estate from the relatively steep climb to Gribben Head help to put the story into context. Thankfully, none of the magic is lost. The eternal surge of the sea and the natural effects of the elements on this stretch of coast give the place a timeless, dreamlike quality.

The climb to Gribben Head offers magnificent views of the twin coves of Polridmouth Bay. Daphne du Maurier and her children often came here to play and picnic.

The waterfront cottage was the inspiration for the boathouse in *Rebecca* where the alluring first Mrs de Winter entertained her lovers, watched through the window by Ben, the local beachcomber.

The crashing waves at the entrance to the bay recall the tragic events in the book and it was here in January 1930 that du Maurier actually witnessed a ship break its back on the rocks. The boathouse cottage in the story can still be seen and nearby is a weather-beaten winch to haul a boat ashore.

On a sunny afternoon, when the shadows of passing clouds darken the landscape for a moment, there is a tangible sense of the book.

Though it is the house, not the heroine, that dominates *Rebecca*, in reality Menabilly is not visible – or at least I couldn't detect it. Try as I might, I could not see 'the grey roof of a house set in its own grounds'. It seems the dense profusion of trees spilling down towards the sea shields it from such prying eyes, but perhaps it is apt that Menabilly itself is not seen, only the setting, the privacy and seclusion helping preserve the mystery of the book. In reality and in du Maurier's fictional world, the house at the centre of the story still doggedly refuses to give up its secrets: 'Last night, I dreamt I went to Manderley again. Nature had encroached upon the drive with long, tenacious fingers. A lilac had mated with a beech, and to bind them more closely, malevolent ivy had thrown her tendrils about the pair.'

Daphne du Maurier 1907–89

Daphne du Maurier's father was the renowned actor-manager Sir Gerald du Maurier and she was born in London. Cornwall, with its rocky grandeur and stunning Atlantic views, lay at the heart of her affections and she used this glorious corner of the country as the setting for many of her highly successful adventure stories and period romances. *Jamaica Inn* (1936), *Frenchman's Creek* (1942), *My Cousin Rachel* (1951) and *The House on the Strand* (1969) are all set in the county.

Her short story *The Birds* (1952) was filmed by Alfred Hitchcock in the USA and became a cinematic classic, while *Don't Look Now* (1970), a macabre short story set in Venice, was filmed by Nicholas Roeg in 1973. Du Maurier also wrote a volume of memoirs – *Vanishing Cornwall* (1967) – among other titles. She married Frederick 'Boy' Browning, who was Deputy Commander of 1st Allied Airborne Division at Arnhem during the Second World War.

THE SOUTH-EAST

KNOLE

THERE IS A STARTLING contrast between the main entrance to Knole and its exquisite parkland setting. One moment you are in a residential street on the outskirts of Sevenoaks, the next, via a narrow gateway where there is often a queue of traffic at the height of summer, you are entering a rarefied world of grazing deer, ancient oak and chestnut trees and undulating grassy clearings.

Eventually the great Elizabethan house looms into view across the rolling Kentish landscape. Surrounded by a glorious thousand-acre park, Knole is one of England's largest houses and the very essence of a grand ancestral seat. Originally an archbishop's palace, gifted to Henry VIII, Knole was given to Thomas Sackville by his cousin, Elizabeth I. There is so much to tell about this ancient, romantic house, not least its fascinating connection with one of Britain's most eminent writers.

Vita Sackville-West grew up at Knole. It captivated and enslaved her to such an extent that there was a time when the house mattered to her more than anything or anyone else. 'I suppose my love for Knole has gone deeper than anything else in my life', she wrote in 1928 when her world suddenly shattered. Her father's death that year changed everything forever. Knole was tied to the Sackville title and could only be inherited down the male line, reflecting the ancient dictates of primogeniture. Sackville-West referred to it as 'a technical fault' but the implications were far greater. The prospect of losing Knole left her inconsolable.

Born Victoria Mary Sackville-West at Knole, she was an only child, and in those formative years she would have known nothing of life apart from a world steeped in history and feudalism and governed by the long-held traditions of the aristocracy.

Knole would have been a playground beyond the wildest dreams of any child. Its sprawling, mediaeval deer park was her back yard and inside the house there were 365 rooms, 52 staircases, 12 entrances and 7 courtyards around which to devise jolly games and fantasy adventures. A curious, secretive child, she loved to explore the house, its secret passages and tantalizing attics, which provided access to the roof.

She once described Knole as a jumble of 'square turrets and grey walls, its hundred chimneys sending blue threads up into the air'. Such was the scale of Knole that in later life her friend and lover Virginia Woolf once estimated that 'the conglomeration of buildings' was probably 'half as big as Cambridge'. Victoria Sackville, Vita's mother, neatly summed up its appeal by claiming it boasted 'the beauties of Windsor Castle and the comforts of The Ritz'.

Sackville-West was eight years of age when Queen Victoria died in 1901. The monarch's passing represented a significant change in British social values and behaviour. It was no different at Knole and the Sackville's young daughter grew up against this startling background of abrupt and immense upheaval.

Vita, was thirty-six years old when Knole passed to her uncle, Major-General Sir Charles Sackville-West, 4th Baron Sackville. Shortly afterwards, Virginia Woolf wrote in her diary: 'I passed Knole with Vita yesterday & had to look away from the vast masterless house, without a flag. This is what she minds most.'

Woolf found Knole cold and uninviting, though she was fascinated by its illustrious ancestry and deep sense of history. She could appreciate Sackville-West's acute feelings of loss. Her lover once eloquently described the house as reflecting 'the tone of England; it melts into the green of the garden turf, into the tawnier green of the park beyond, into the blue of the pale English sky'. To lose what she believed was rightfully hers was like a dagger tearing at her heart. Crucially she saw it as 'a betrayal of all the tradition of my ancestors and the house I loved'.

Sackville-West could never entirely let go of Knole, but Woolf's exceptional gift as a writer found a way to preserve its memory for her, not in reality but in her extraordinary imagination. That same year – 1928 – Woolf wrote a semi-biographical novel *Orlando*, described by Sackville-West's son, Nigel Nicolson, as 'the longest and most charming love letter in literature'. The book draws heavily on the history of Knole and Sackville-West was 'dazzled, bewitched, enchanted' by it – indeed the time-travelling, transgender central character is the embodiment of herself. *Orlando* was an incredible gesture of kindness, an act of love from a woman to whom Sackville-West reciprocated these feelings.

Their affair was passionate and Sackville-West was even slightly overawed by the writer and her irresistible spirit. Woolf was caring and protective in return. 'She shines in the grocer's shop in Sevenoaks with a candle-lit radiance', she wrote. 'Stalking on legs like beech trees, pink glowing, grape clustered, pearl hung. That is the secret of her glamour, I suppose.'

Over the generations, many distinguished guests passed through the gates of Knole. Among them was a woman who would change the course of history. In 1931–2, American divorcee Wallis Simpson was a frequent guest at the house. Her visits stopped abruptly, however, when it became apparent that she was the mistress of the Prince of Wales, the future monarch.

A year before Mrs Simpson first set foot on Knole's soil, in the spring of 1930, Sackville-West completed her own love letter to the house where she had grown up. *The Edwardians* was the writer's most successful book and although it is a work of fiction, the author's note states: 'No character in this book is wholly fictitious.' It is a telling statement.

Much had changed in the country and throughout the world in the nearly thirty years since Queen Victoria's death, and *The Edwardians* touches on aspects of that social revolution. The novel is set at Chevron, a country house clearly inspired by Knole. The story begins in 1905 and concludes in 1911, a year after Edward VII's death and three years before the start of the Great War. Influenced by her own childhood experiences at Knole, the book is about the life Sackville-West knew best – a world inhabited by the upper ranks of aristocratic society. Interestingly, although she was born into that world, she classed herself as Bohemian and unconventional. One of her characters in *The Edwardians* describes

Chevron as 'a dead thing; an anachronism, an exquisite survival'.

It wasn't the first time Vita Sackville-West had written about Knole. Between 1906 and 1910, while in her mid-teens, she produced eight novels and five plays. Invariably, she wrote in the summerhouse and Knole's eclectic history and its many occupants over the centuries were her inspiration.

Despite the gift of *Orlando*, intended to assuage the heartache brought about by the loss of her beloved Knole, Sackville-West was haunted by images of the house for the rest of her life. In a letter to her husband, Harold Nicolson, written on 16 May 1928, she wrote:

> I allowed myself a torture-treat last night: I went up to Knole after dark and wandered about in the garden. I have a master key, so could get in without being seen. It was a very queer and poignant experience; so queer and poignant, that I should have fainted had I met anybody. I mean, I had the sensation of having the place so completely to myself, that I might have been the only person alive in the world – and not the world of today, mark you, but the world of at least 300 years ago.

The nocturnal experience may well have been akin to a romantic interlude, a rendezvous with an old lover. No doubt for a few brief minutes the magic returned and the memories swam.

Of the garden at Knole, Sackville-West once wrote: 'The turf is the most brilliant green; there is a sound of bees in the limes; the heat grows like watered gauze above the ridge of the lawn. The high wall of rag [Kentish ragstone] round the garden gives a curious sense of seclusion and quiet.'

In 1940, as war raged in Europe, the biographer and travel writer James Pope Hennessy, on a visit to Knole, wrote: 'We walked in the great dark gardens in the evening light with wide turf alleys and rhododendron flowers ... but it was only an illusion of peace and the previous tranquil world, and the whole ordered landscape seemed quivering with imminent destruction.'

By the early years of the Second World War Knole was struggling to support itself. In 1946, the 4th Baron Sackville gave the house and an endowment for its upkeep to the National Trust. Two years later Vita Sackville-West wrote the first National Trust guidebook to Knole.

SISSINGHURST CASTLE

IT MAY NOT HAVE been as grand as Knole – the ancestral home which, by the anachronistic rules of primogeniture, Vita Sackville-West was denied – but as consolation prizes go, Sissinghurst Castle wasn't a bad choice. Sackville-West recorded in her diary:

> When I first saw it on a spring day in 1930, it caught instantly at my heart and my imagination. I fell flat in love with it; love at first sight. I saw what might be made of it. It was Sleeping Beauty's Castle; but a castle running away into sordidness and squalor, a garden crying out for rescue. It was easy to foresee, even then, what a struggle we should have to redeem it.

Originally an impressive late fifteenth-century courtyard house built by the Baker family and substantially enlarged in the 1560s, all that remained of Sissinghurst at the time Sackville-West and her husband Harold Nicolson acquired it were the mellowed pink brick ruins of the Tudor outbuildings. Most striking among this collection is the prominent tower gateway that once fronted the great house.

The start of the couple's new life at Sissinghurst was hardly auspicious. For the first few nights, conditions were primitive and they slept on camp beds, reading only by candlelight. The garden beyond was a wilderness of brambles, broken fencing and long-discarded items of rubbish, including sardine tins, bedsteads and plough-shares. Unable to conceal the bitterness she still felt following her disinheritance, Sackville-West wrote:

> One might reasonably have hoped to inherit century-old hedges of yew, some gnarled mulberries, a cedar or two, a pleached alley, flagged walks, a mound. Instead there was nothing but weed,

rough grass, a shabby eyesore of a greenhouse in the wrong place, broken fencing, wired chicken runs, squalor and slovenly disorder everywhere.

The challenge of transforming Sissinghurst's sketchy remains was a formidable one but Nicolson and Sackville-West laboured long and hard – very much as a business partnership. She gardened while he designed. The layout by Nicolson and the planting by Sackville-West were evidently influenced by the work of Gertrude Jekyll and Edwin Lutyens and by Lawrence Johnston's Edwardian Garden at Hidcote in Gloucestershire, which they greatly admired.

In 1938, Vita Sackville-West reluctantly opened Sissinghurst to the public. She rather haughtily dubbed its visitors as 'the shillingses', a reference to the admission charge, which then was one shilling (5p). Today, the fee is inevitably greater but visitors are treated to a treasure-trove of horticultural delights. The fruits of Nicolson's and Sackville-West's hugely ambitious labour of love are their legacy.

For Sackville-West, Sissinghurst's attraction lay not just in the garden and the potential to create a series of intimate open-air rooms using old walls and hedges. The tower gateway became the pivotal point of her life as a writer; it was her retreat, lying at the heart of her private world of books and journalism. Intensely private and independent, Sackville-West was fiercely protective of her work-place. Visitors were not welcome.

Halfway up the tower and reached by a spiral staircase, the writing room remains unchanged, its walls still lined with long-forgotten publications on subjects such as gardening, history and travel. On long summer days Sackville-West would garden until dusk and then disappear to her desk, writing for hours into the night. She wrote twenty books in her dearly loved eyrie, and between 1946 and 1961 she produced a much-anticipated weekly gardening column for the *Observer*.

Electricity was eventually installed in the tower and a brick fireplace built, though Sackville-West rarely lit it. Instead, she would wear extra layers of clothing or use blankets to keep warm. Sometimes she would switch on an electric fire, though usually she restricted its use to one bar.

Sackville-West loved to climb to the top of the tower and gaze down at the fruits of her labours – her cherished garden. Her gaze would then fix on the wider view: the patchwork of fields and woods stretching to the distant ridge of the North Downs. The spire of Frittenden Church, nestling in the middle distance, was a reassuring reminder of all that was good about her beloved Garden of England.

When the peace and calm of that very English landscape was threatened by enemy forces in 1940, Sackville-West moved to another study in order to accommodate members of the Observer Corps, who used the top of the tower for surveillance.

Sissinghurst's library, also open to visitors, contains thousands of books, many of which were Harold Nicolson's review copies. He wrote at South Cottage, part of Sissinghurst, a more conventional workplace, while his wife sought peace and privacy in her tower writing room. Ironically, he was the more prolific writer at Sissinghurst, recording three million words for his daily diary, produced on one of his three typewriters, known as Rikki, Tikki and Tavi, 'without thought of publication'.

Although a wealthy woman when she moved to Sissinghurst, Sackville-West was virtually penniless by the time she died, her personal fortune having been spent on her home and garden and countless hours devoted to fulfilling her dream. Sissinghurst 'broke my back, my fingernails and sometimes my heart', she wrote.

After her death the estate passed to the National Trust in lieu of death duties and today nine gardeners are employed to maintain and protect her creation.

In 1973, Nigel Nicolson, Sackville-West's son, wrote a memoir, *Portrait of a Marriage*, based on a manuscript found in a locked Gladstone bag in the tower at Sissinghurst Castle and written by Nicolson's mother when she was twenty-eight. Poignantly, the writing was intended to lay to rest Sackville-West's deep, overpowering feelings for another woman, Violet Trefusis, a noted writer and socialite.

Though Vita Sackville-West died over half a century ago, the literary link at Sissinghurst has been gloriously maintained. Her grandson, Adam Nicolson, a respected and established writer himself, lives at Sissinghurst Castle with his family and has cherished memories of growing up on the estate.

As a five-year-old, in the early 1960s, he would race through the gardens on his tricycle, starting under the big arch, then cutting across the main lawn, through the rose garden and the spring garden, finishing at the herb garden. He would proudly complete the course in little under one minute. But young Adam didn't exactly have Sissinghurst to himself. He was used to sharing the garden and grounds with about 25,000 visitors a year.

Nicolson still takes a occasional bicycle trip round the grounds. Memories flood back and by late afternoon, with the gates firmly closed for the day, the place seems eerily quiet, reminding him of his privileged position and the extraordinary woman who wrote here and, against all the odds, created a unique garden in the ruins of a beautiful house. 'We have done our best,' Sackville-West wrote to her husband just before she died, 'and made a garden where none was.'

Vita (Victoria) Sackville-West 1892–1962

Born at Knole and educated privately, Vita Sackville-West won the Hawthornden Prize for her long, masterly poem *The Land* (1927). Her most famous novels, including *The Edwardians* (1930) and *All Passion Spent* (1931), deal with themes of privilege and inherited wealth. She also wrote an account of her illustrious family in *Knole and the Sackvilles* (1947), while *Passenger to Tehran* (1926) concentrates on her time in Persia with her husband, the diplomat Harold Nicolson, whom she married in 1913. Her unorthodox 'open marriage' allowed her to conduct affairs with women, including a passionate relationship with Violet Trefusis, though Nicolson's bisexuality and her dalliances failed to destroy what was seen as a strong and enduring partnership.

GREAT MAYTHAM HALL
(Garden access only)

FOR MANY READERS, FRANCES Hodgson Burnett's children's literary classic *The Secret Garden* evokes nostalgic memories of endless dreamy summers and glorious country house settings. A visit to the garden at Great Maytham Hall, a splendid Grade II house in the depths of the Kent countryside, goes one step further to reawaken in us images of the childhood world of our own imagination. The garden inspired this much-loved story, set in Yorkshire and published in 1911.

Hodgson Burnett was tenant of Great Maytham Hall between 1898 and 1907. Among its distinguished visitors were many leading literary and theatrical figures of the day, including Rudyard Kipling, Ellen Terry and Henry James, who lived at nearby Rye. Typically, as a writer, Hodgson Burnett was constantly inspired by what she saw around her. One day, while in the garden at Great Maytham, her attention was captured by a solitary robin, leading her to discover a door concealed by ivy in one of the garden's characteristic mellow brick walls. On the other side of the door lay an overgrown eighteenth-century garden, which Hodgson Burnett transformed. With the help of the hall's head gardener, she expanded the view of the lawns, planted numerous flowers and constructed a rose walkway. Hodgson Burnett's stroke of good fortune led her to produce her most enduring work, *The Secret Garden*, although she had departed Great Maytham by the time the book was published.

The neglected walled garden discovered by Frances Hodgson Burnett dated back to 1721 and was part of the original Georgian house.

After nine blissful years as its tenant, Hodgson Burnett was informed that Great Maytham Hall was to be sold. She could afford to rent the house, but not to buy it. Her time there was over. She wrote to her sister:

> It was living at Maytham which meant England to me, in a way … that place belongs to me – it is the only place I ever felt was home…. It seemed a sort of outrage that I was not living there. It seemed so what one needed – that sense of being able to go out of one big room into another – to go down corridors into room after room – to go upstairs and walk about.

The Secret Garden has spanned the decades and the generations with its charming story of how two children are transformed by the discovery of a secret garden, which becomes an integral part of their lives. They watch transfixed as the garden bursts into life, weaving its magic on all who enter it. Not surprisingly, Hodgson Burnett's best-known work has been adapted for the cinema. *The Secret Garden* is told in three film adaptations, the first being a silent version and the most recent released in 1993. In the latter, lavishly filmed on location around the country, the book's Gothic atmosphere is largely preserved and there is a typically memorable performance by Maggie Smith as the tyrannical housekeeper.

Great Maytham Hall may have long been associated with one of the greatest examples of children's literature, but there is a good deal more to its story. The present house, designed and remodelled by Sir Edwin Lutyens, is as old as Hodgson Burnett's book, standing on the site of a previous eighteenth-century building and including part of it.

Lutyens worked closely with the horticulturalist Gertrude Jekyll, who was responsible for designing and landscaping the grounds. The original building, which was begun in 1721 and remained roofless through lack of funds until 1760, had strong links with myriad myths and legends. According to some sources the house boasted a smugglers' tunnel, while others claimed a ghost had been witnessed rising from a nearby pond.

The present house was commissioned by John Tennant, Liberal

Described as 'one of the finest buildings in Kent', Great Maytham Hall was designed by Lutyens and dates back to 1909. The house became the setting for the General Headquarters of the French forces in the British war film *Dunkirk*, made in 1958.

Member of Parliament for Berwickshire, who invited Lutyens to construct a family home commensurate with his status. Lutyens accepted the challenge, transforming the old house, which had been partially destroyed by fire in 1893. Working with Jekyll, he ensured that the principal rooms took advantage of the south-westerly views of Great Maytham's grounds and the fertile countryside of the Rother Valley.

Tennant lived at Great Maytham Hall from 1909 until his death in 1935. During the Second World War, the Army requisitioned the house and Great Maytham Hall became a billet for the Medical Corps. One day a bomb fell on the estate, narrowly missing the main house but destroying the greenhouses and part of the garden. Photographs show soldiers repairing the damage.

By the mid-1950s, following a succession of owners, the house had fallen into disrepair. The grounds, too, were in a sorry state, with weeds and brambles threatening to engulf what had been Great Maytham's pride and joy – its treasured garden. Its miraculous rescue recalls Hodgson Burnett's magical tale.

After the Second World War the garden at Great Maytham Hall was largely overgrown.
Brambles took hold while the lower lawn was let for grazing. Two irreplaceable Irish yews,
considered a danger to livestock, were felled.

In 1955 the landscape architect Anthony Du Gard Pasley missed
his turning in Rolvenden and, looking for a suitable gateway
in which to reverse his car, found himself gazing down Great
Maytham's stately drive at the derelict house and its overgrown
garden. He couldn't believe what he saw. Here was a Lutyens
masterpiece – ravaged by time and the elements, abandoned and
unloved. When Du Gard Pasley discovered that a planning application had been made to demolish Great Maytham Hall and build
houses on the site, he led a successful campaign to reject the plans.
Great Maytham Hall and its wondrous garden were secure.

In 1961 the estate was acquired by the Mutual Households
Association, which later became the Country Houses Association.
The house was converted into apartments for members of the armed
forces returning to Britain. Today, Great Maytham is owned and
managed by the Sunley Group.

The world of Frances Hodgson Burnett has changed almost
beyond recognition since she lived at Great Maytham Hall, but
the place survives. Here, in the old walled rose garden, on warm

summer days, she would set up her table, chair and protective sunshade. She always wore a white dress and a large hat. When it rained she would retreat to the comfort of the gazebo.

More than a century later, the same walled garden continues to evoke the magic of her writing. Visitors view it at its best during the summer months and couples choose it as a venue for civil marriage ceremonies. When the crowds disperse, this enchanting plot, once the outdoor workplace of a renowned Anglo-American writer, once again assumes the atmosphere of a secret garden largely undisturbed by the modern world.

Frances Hodgson Burnett 1849–1924

Born in Manchester, the daughter of a manufacturer, Frances Hodgson Burnett emigrated to America with her family when she was sixteen. On arrival in Knoxville, Tennessee, she began writing, principally to help the family finances. She married in 1873, though the relationship was not a happy one and the couple divorced in 1898. She returned to Britain frequently throughout her life and, following her death, a memorial to her in the form of a statue of a boy and a girl was erected in Central Park, New York. Apart from *The Secret Garden*, her best-known work is *Little Lord Fauntleroy* (1886). By the end of her life, Frances Hodgson Burnett had produced fifty-two novels and thirteen plays. Most of her output was written for adults. She died in New York.

DICKENS HOUSE MUSEUM

THE ARTIST JOSEPH TURNER claimed that the Isle of Thanet enjoyed the loveliest skies in Europe and the writer John Buchan set the final chapter of his classic spy adventure *The Thirty-Nine Steps* (1915) in this picturesque corner of Kent. The inspiration for the novel came from a holiday Buchan spent in Broadstairs the previous summer. Military historian Sir John Keegan writes in his introduction to a recent edition of the book: 'Buchan was drawing directly on the scenes that lay about him.'

Charles Dickens, too, drew directly on the scenes that lay about him and his knowledge of Broadstairs when he wrote *David*

Copperfield, published in 1849–50 and considered to be his most autobiographical novel. Dickens visited the popular seaside resort for the first time in 1837. He was only twenty-five at the time but already recognized as a writer of merit. He loved Broadstairs and he and his family spent their annual summer holiday here between 1839 and 1851. He referred to the town as his 'English Watering-Place'.

Dickens spent many summers in Broadstairs, taking a house in the town or staying in a local hotel. He regarded the place as the quintessentially English holiday resort. From 1853 the Dickens family holidayed in France.

It was Miss Mary Pearson Strong who inspired Dickens to create the character of Betsey Trotwood, David Copperfield's great-aunt, in the story. Strong lived in Broadstairs and she and the burgeoning novelist developed their friendship during his holiday visits. He would call on Trotwood and watch her chase away the donkey-boys who repeatedly rode across the green in front of her home. Although Dickens moved Trotwood's home to Dover in the story, possibly to spare his friend any embarrassment, it is clearly based on Strong's cottage in Broadstairs.

Situated in Victoria Parade in Broadstairs, the Dickens House Museum retains the character and appearance of the former home of Miss Mary Pearson Strong, a friend of Dickens, especially on the ground floor.

In Chapter 13 of *David Copperfield*, Dickens refers to 'a very neat little cottage with cheerful bow-windows: in front of it, a small square gravelled court or garden full of flowers, carefully tended, and smelling deliciously'. Dickens makes much of Strong's persistent battle with the unruly donkey-boys in the chapter. His son, Charley, recalled that she was utterly convinced of her right to stop the their relentless passage in front of her home. Copperfield notes:

> To this hour I don't know whether my aunt had any lawful right of way over that patch of green; but she had settled it in her own mind that she had, and it was all the same to her. The one great outrage of her life, demanding to be constantly avenged, was the passage of a donkey over that immaculate spot.... Jugs of water, and watering-pots, were kept in secret places ready to be discharged on the offending boys; sticks were laid in ambush behind the door; sallies were made at all hours; and incessant war prevailed ... I saw my aunt engage, single-handed, with a sandy-haired lad of fifteen, and bump his sandy head against her own gate, before he seemed to comprehend what was the matter.

Betsey Trotwood is portrayed in *David Copperfield* as an eccentric and reclusive benefactor. She was married but her husband's cruel nature led her to leave him and resume her maiden name. When young Copperfield appears at her cottage, she adopts him as her son and changes his name to Trotwood Copperfield. The boy describes his great-aunt as 'a tall, hard-featured lady, but by no means ill-looking ... I particularly noticed that she had a very quick, bright eye'. Although initially austere, Trotwood gradually softens as she and Copperfield grow closer and, in old age, she relishes his success as an author.

Miss Pearson Strong's former home became known as Dickens House in the closing years of the nineteenth century. Details of its subsequent occupants are patchy, though it is known that the Tattam family acquired the house in 1919 and in 1973 it opened to the public for the first time. The original building is part Tudor with later additions, while much of the present house dates back to the late Georgian period. The balcony is Victorian. The ground floor includes Trotwood's parlour, where Dickens took tea with Pearson Strong on many occasions. The room is furnished in accordance with Dickens's description as seen through the eyes of David Copperfield and recreated with the help of English Heritage from the illustration by Phiz, which appears in the book with the caption: 'The Momentous Interview'.

> The room was as neat as Janet or my aunt. As I laid down my pen, a moment since, to think of it, the air from the sea came blowing in again, mixed with the perfume of the flowers; and I saw the old-fashioned furniture brightly rubbed and polished, my aunt's inviolable chair and table by the round green fan in the bow-window, the drugget-covered carpet, the cat, the kettle-holder, the two canaries, the old china, the punch-bowl full of dried rose-leaves, the tall press guarding all sorts of bottles and pots, and, wonderfully out of keeping with the rest, my dusty self upon the sofa, taking note of everything.

In the parlour is the cupboard acknowledged as the 'press' from which Trotwood produces the concoctions she pours down David

Copperfield's throat after he arrives at her home in an agitated state, having run away from London:

> she got up in a great hurry, collared me, and took me into the parlour. Her first proceeding there was to unlock a tall press, bring out several bottles, and pour some of the contents of each into my mouth. I think they must have been taken out at random, for I am sure I tasted aniseed water, anchovy sauce and salad dressing. When she had administered these restoratives, as I was still quite hysterical, and unable to control my sobs, she put me on the sofa, with a shawl under my head, and the handkerchief from her own head under my feet, lest I should sully the cover.

RESTORATION HOUSE

PROMINENT IN THE GALLERY of wildly exaggerated characters created by Charles Dickens is the doomed and tragic figure of Miss Havisham. The author's portrait is of a desperate, tormented woman, jilted on her wedding day, lost and alone in her decaying home – now a sorry tangle of cobwebs and overrun with vermin. In typical fashion, Dickens paints a heartbreaking picture, leaving the reader with an acute, overwhelming sense of sadness.

Satis House, Miss Havisham's eerie home in *Great Expectations* (1860–1), is modelled on Restoration House in Rochester. Dickens knew the city well. He made it his home in 1856 and many of Rochester's finest buildings recall its links with the novelist who is the most widely known English writer after Shakespeare.

Restoration House originally comprised two mediaeval wings dating back to the mid-fifteenth and early sixteenth centuries. Between 1640 and 1660 they became one property when the two houses were joined together by a new hall and screens passage built in the mediaeval style. The Great Chamber, which was 'Miss Havisham's room', was built above. Further work was undertaken in about 1670 when the present façade was added to the hall and an intriguing jumble of staircases and doorways created.

'There is no finer pre-Civil War town house than this in England',

Evidently, Charles Dickens was familiar with the interior of Restoration House. In *Great Expectations*, the room in which Charles II spent the night becomes Miss Havisham's bedroom and the drawing room across the landing is where he places her decaying wedding breakfast.

wrote the journalist Simon Jenkins in *The Times* in 2001.

This fine Elizabethan redbrick mansion, located just outside the south-east corner of the city wall, acquired its name after the visit of Charles II on the eve of his Restoration. He lodged here on his return to England in May 1660. Charles landed at Dover and by evening he was in Rochester. He continued to London the following day, where he reclaimed the crown.

Though Satis House is the name Dickens gave to Miss Havisham's home in *Great Expectations*, he used artistic licence to disguise its real identity, taking the name from a house in Rochester, which was once the home of Richard Watts, a mayor of the city, and where Elizabeth I once stayed as his guest. Watts apparently apologized to the monarch for the modesty of his home, to which she replied '*satis*' – Latin for 'it is enough'. Today, Satis House is home to the administrative offices of the King's School, Rochester.

In his introduction to a recent edition of *Great Expectations*, Dr John Bowen describes Miss Havisham's home as 'exactly where one might expect a semi-deranged woman to live – dark, miserable, decaying – it also seems like a place out of a fairy-tale or a Gothic novel, somewhere that comes from our deepest dreams and fancies'.

Dickens himself first draws our attention to Satis House in Chapter 8 of *Great Expectations* with the arrival of Pip:

> Within a quarter of an hour we came to Miss Havisham's house, which was of old brick, and dismal, and had a great many iron bars to it. Some of the windows had been walled up; of those that remained, all the lower were rustily barred. There was a courtyard in front, and that was barred; so, we had to wait, after ringing the bell, until someone should come to open it.

Later in the story Pip, believing that his task is to 'restore the desolate house, admit the sunshine into the dark rooms, set the clocks a-going and the cold hearths a-blazing, tear down the cobwebs, destroy the vermin – in short, do all the shining deeds of the young Knight of romance' passes Satis House and gazes up at 'its seared red brick walls, blocked windows and strong green ivy clasping even the stacks of chimneys with its twigs and tendons.'

It is claimed that Charles Dickens was seen leaning against the main gate to Restoration House the day before he died. Its name is

apt. It has been revived and restored by different owners over the centuries and today it has the air and atmosphere of a family home rather than a city museum.

Close to Restoration House stands the Swiss Chalet, presented to Dickens by a friend. He worked on the upper floor where he installed mirrors to reflect the light. He wrote 'My room is up among the branches of the trees; and the birds and butterflies fly in and out.'

'Ours was the marsh country down by the river, within, as the river wound, 20 miles of the sea,' wrote Dickens in the first chapter of *Great Expectations*. In places, these bleak Kent marshes still convey the dark, malevolent atmosphere of the book.

In his writing, Dickens creates a vivid picture of the Thames Estuary as it was in the mid-nineteenth century – a place of brooding horizons and shipping beacons and, emerging through the mist, the ghostly outlines of the convict ships.

Charles Dickens 1812–70

Born in Portsmouth, the son of a clerk in the Navy pay office at the city's dockyard, Charles Dickens was the second of eight children. He outlived them all except his sister, Letitia, who died in 1893. The family later moved to Chatham and then London, where Dickens senior experienced financial difficulties and served time at a debtors' prison.

After a period of childhood employment at a blacking factory on London's Embankment, young Dickens worked as a journalist at the House of Commons and subsequently for the newspaper trade, contributing papers and sketches to the *Evening Chronicle* and the *Morning Chronicle*. He adopted the pen name 'Boz'. *Sketches by Boz* were collected and published in 1836; that year he married Catherine Hogarth who bore him seven sons and three daughters. Three of the children predeceased their father. Dickens and Catherine separated in 1858.

Dickens's career as a respected and much-loved author began in 1836 with the publication of *The Pickwick Papers*. Other titles include *Oliver Twist* (1837–9), *Hard Times* (1854) and *A Tale of Two Cities* (1859). Dickens spent his later years at Gad's Hill Place, his beloved Georgian home near Rochester. He embarked on speaking tours and public readings of his work in Britain and North America and at the time of his death, aged fifty-eight, following a stroke, he was working on his unfinished novel *The Mystery of Edwin Drood*.

GREAT DIXTER

IN TODAY'S CELEBRITY-OBSESSED WORLD even gardeners are often household names. Not so the gardening writer Christopher Lloyd, who died in 2006. Although hugely admired and respected in horticultural circles and by his many readers, he never gained celebrity status and almost certainly would have baulked at the idea if he had.

Acknowledged as the doyen of gardening experts by those who knew and read him, Lloyd's name was synonymous with Great Dixter, his much-loved family home and birthplace in East Sussex. Built in the middle of the fifteenth century and later restored and enlarged by Sir Edwin Lutyens, Great Dixter was an integral part of Lloyd's life, as was its garden, which has given pleasure to thousands of visitors over the years.

In partnership with Nathaniel Lloyd, the then owner, Sir Edwin Lutyens transformed Great Dixter and also redesigned the garden, establishing topiary yews to create 'rooms'. His influence is unmistakable.

Lloyd spent many hours completing different outdoor projects. He established natural ponds and designed yew topiary – among many other notable horticultural features. The result is one of the most exciting, colourful and constantly changing gardens of modern times.

Lutyens, too, brought his unique style and influence to bear in the garden of Great Dixter. Typically inventive, he often used tiles in a decorative though practical manner, to great effect. He even took a ruined chicken house and transformed it into an open-sided loggia, supported by laminated tile pillars.

Christopher Lloyd's father, Nathaniel, was an Arts and Crafts designer. Nathaniel acquired Great Dixter in 1910, instructing Lutyens to make major changes to the house, which at that time was in a poor state of repair. His chief objective was to rid Great Dixter of later alterations, a task Lutyens completed with great sensitivity.

However, the work didn't stop there. While the restoration work was beginning to take shape, he and Nathaniel seized the chance

Set peacefully in the Sussex Weald, Great Dixter draws visitors from far and wide. The garden is a haven for horticulturalists while the fascinating Tudor interior of the ancient house attracts many architectural historians.

to enlarge the house. A complete timber-framed yeoman's hall at nearby Benenden, across the county border in Kent, was painstakingly dismantled piece by piece and moved to Great Dixter, adding an entire wing.

Today, first-time visitors to the house are overwhelmed by its striking features – in particular the magnificent Great Hall, which is the largest surviving timber-framed hall in the country, renowned for its mediaeval splendour. The half-timbered and plastered front and the Tudor porch also catch the eye. Great Dixter's contents date mainly from the seventeenth and eighteenth centuries and were collected over the years by Nathaniel Lloyd. He died in 1933, leaving the 450-acre estate to his widow Daisy, a descendant of Oliver Cromwell.

During the mid-1950s, Christopher Lloyd established a nursery at Great Dixter specializing in unusual and uncommon plants. The writer Vita Sackville-West (*see* Knole and Sissinghurst Castle) gave him cuttings of the plant, Rosemary Corsican Blue.

Lloyd and his mother both loved gardening and were practical gardeners. Together they sought new ideas, which often presented fresh challenges, in an effort to preserve and enhance what many consider to be a jewel among country house gardens. Their partnership and shared passion for horticulture lasted until Daisy's death in 1972. Renowned for his radical views, Lloyd was firmly rooted in the Arts and Crafts style of garden. 'I couldn't design a garden,' he once said, 'I just go along and carp.'

In the late 1950s Lloyd wrote the first of a number of books, which dwelt on the theme of gardening. In 1963 he began working for *Country Life*, writing a weekly column called 'In my Garden.' The articles were published over a lengthy period lasting more than forty years. He was also, until his death, gardening correspondent of the *Guardian*.

Lloyd also wrote about food. Cooking was one of his great pleasures – especially when it involved home-grown fruit and vegetables. Inspired by his mother and by Jane Grigson and Delia Smith, among others, he became an expert cook – hardly surprising given his inherent creative skills and quirky, gregarious nature. He preferred to serve straight from the stove and abhorred cookery

As a gardener, Christopher Lloyd – or 'Christo' as he was known – was daring and innovative. His weekly gardening column in *Country Life* was testament to his knowledge of horticulture, as well as a voice for his views and ideas on the subject.

books with 'glamorously laid-out meals and violently coloured illustration'.

Lloyd's love of life was reflected in the daily routine at Great Dixter. There were frequent parties and all manner of houseguests. Life was never dull. On one occasion Lloyd's dachshunds ate the sandwiches of a party of visiting Hungarians who were studying horticulture. To remedy the situation he invited them to stay at Great Dixter. Other students and overseas visitors could be found camped on the floor of the Great Hall in their sleeping bags.

Christopher Lloyd continued to live at Great Dixter in his latter years. It became impossible to picture him anywhere else. He loved the house and especially the garden where, dressed in corduroys and an old jumper, trug by his side, he spent many happy and contented hours.

Christopher Lloyd 1921–2006

Christopher Lloyd attended Rugby and King's College, Cambridge, where he read modern languages. After war service in the Army he received his Bachelor in Decorative Horticulture (design and planning) from Wye College, part of the University of London. He stayed on as assistant lecturer in horticulture until 1954. He produced his first book, *The Mixed Border*, in 1957, following a lengthy period developing and nurturing Great Dixter's famous long border. The book was the direct result of Lloyd's desire to share his thoughts and experiences with fellow gardeners. Two further books followed in 1965, both now considered modern minor classics: *Clematis* (co-written with John Treasure) and *Trees and Shrubs for Small Gardens*. In all, Lloyd wrote over twenty books, including *The Well-tempered Garden* (1970) and *The Gardener Cook* (1997), and his lengthy correspondence with fellow gardener Beth Chatto was published in 1998 as *Dear Friend and Gardener*. His final gardening title, *Exotic Planting for Adventurous Gardeners*, was published posthumously in 2007.

LAMB HOUSE

BUILT BY JAMES LAMB, a former long-term mayor of the picturesque old Cinque Port of Rye, Lamb House first sprang to prominence only three years after construction work was finished. George I spent four nights at the house in 1726 after being shipwrecked nearby en route to London to open Parliament. In his official capacity as mayor, and with his wife about to give birth, Lamb rushed to the aid of the stranded king, offering him his own bedroom at Lamb House. Not surprisingly, the couple's newborn son was named George.

Four years after the American writer Henry James first set eyes on Lamb House, which he later made his home, he received a visit from a fellow author, E.F. Benson, whose name was less familiar to the reading public at that time than that of James. When they met, neither man could possibly have envisaged that one day the world of literature would recall that this delightful house, built in 1723 and situated in a large walled garden, on the corner of a narrow cobbled street, was occupied by both of them, though in markedly contrasting periods.

On signing the lease on Lamb House, Henry James wrote to E.F. Benson's elder brother, Arthur: 'But it is exactly what I want, and secretly and hopelessly coveted (since knowing it) without dreaming it would ever fall.'

It was in 1896 that James's love affair with Lamb House began, although initially its enchantment was largely fuelled by his own imagination. He had first seen the house when it was no more than the subject of a watercolour in the London home of an architect friend. Over several subsequent summers, while on holiday in Sussex, he could be found 'casting sheep's eyes at Lamb House'. Rye in general and Lamb House in particular had cast their spell on him.

Soon, James was considering the idea of making the town his permanent home. When, in 1898, he discovered by great good fortune that the owner had died and Lamb House was available to rent, he wasted no time in purchasing the lease 'on quite deliciously moderate terms'. He bought the freehold a year later, paying £2,000 for it.

Clearly James had no regrets about his decision to move to Rye, writing 'all the good that I hoped of the place has, in fine, properly bloomed and flourished here … the quite essential amiability of Lamb House only deepens with experience'. James's devotion to the place was such that he once declared he was prepared to offer 'the whole bristling state of Connecticut' in exchange for one brick from the wall of his garden. Much more than just bricks and mortar, Lamb House was his 'russet Arcadia'.

James adhered to a strict routine at Lamb House. He would write for three or four hours every morning in his garden workroom, built in the mid-eighteenth century as a banqueting house to the main house. A bow window topped with a pediment offered a striking view of Rye's churchyard and the heart of the town. (Sadly, a German bomb destroyed the Garden Room in the summer of 1940.) James did not welcome interruption during these productive working hours and in Benson's memoir, *Final Edition,* the writer describes James's voice 'booming and pausing and booming again, as he moved up and down the book-lined room dictating the novel on which he was at work to his typist'. In middle age, ill health – most notably a repetitive strain injury – forced James to abandon writing his novels by hand.

During the winter months James wrote in the main house, using a small study on the first floor. Some of his best-known and most important literary work, including the novels *The Wings of the Dove* (1902), *The Ambassadors* (1903) and *The Golden Bowl* (1904) was written at Lamb House, which, during James's tenure, witnessed a steady stream of established fellow writers passing through its portal. H.G. Wells, Rudyard Kipling, Joseph Conrad and Hilaire Belloc were among the many visitors. Guests often travelled to Rye by train and were met at the station, their luggage transported through the quaint, cobbled streets to Lamb House in a wheelbarrow.

Henry James was a familiar figure in Rye, often seen out walking with his dachshund or meeting his guests off the train. His close friend, the writer Edith Wharton, wrote: 'Some of my richest hours were spent under his roof.'

Eighteen years after Lamb House captured his heart, Henry James entered a phase of his life that would be overshadowed by failing health and the shattering effects of war. In the autumn of 1914, against this stark background and unsettled by Rye's insidious damp winters, James left Lamb House for the last time and moved to London.

*

E.F. (Fred) Benson first came to stay at Lamb House in 1900. His brother, A.C. (Arthur) Benson, was a friend of Henry James. He was equally charmed by the property and, following James's death during the First World War, Benson made regular visits to Lamb House as the guest of George Plank, a friend of the then tenant, Mrs Beevor, who stayed at the house for prolonged periods when Beevor was away wintering on the Riviera.

The lease of Lamb House was offered to Fred Benson and his brother Arthur, master of Magdalen College, Cambridge, in 1919. They found an amicable way of arranging their time there: Fred lived there in term time and Arthur during the vacation. After his brother's death in 1925, Fred became Mayor of Rye from 1934–7, following in the tradition of James Lamb. He chose not to buy the freehold of Lamb House, which now belonged to Henry James's nephew, citing as the main reasons his lack of direct descendants and the long lease on his London home.

A prolific author, best known for the Mapp and Lucia novels, Benson made great use of Rye in his writing. In the books he changed its name to Tilling, but in just about every other respect Rye is immediately identifiable as the town of his imagination. The clues confirm it. Mermaid Street is Porpoise Street and Watchbell Street becomes Curfew Street. A keen ornithologist, Benson renamed Lamb House in the stories, calling it Mallards. He also made it the home of the formidable Miss Mapp and then Lucia. The novels, representing an exaggerated, caricatured study of upper middle-class English society, with its cultural snobbery and petty hypocrisy, were championed by many eminent writers of the period, including Nancy Mitford, Noël Coward and W.H. Auden.

Having lived at Rye for twenty years, Benson became ill at the end of 1939 and died several months later in London. Lamb House passed to the National Trust after the war, though its particularly strong association with the literary world continued well into the second half of the twentieth century. Between 1967 and 1973 it was let to the novelist and children's author Rumer Godden (1907–98).

Henry James 1843–1916

The son of a respected theological writer and lecturer, Henry James was born in Manhattan. After studying law at Harvard, he began to produce acclaimed literary reviews and short stories. He settled in London in the 1870s and wrote some of his best-known work while living there, including *The Portrait of a Lady* (1881) and *The Bostonians* (1886). His themes dealt mainly with the impact of American life on the older European civilization and the darker recesses of political life in Europe. His second phase of literary work began just before the turn of the century and focused exclusively on English subjects. *The Ambassadors* (1903) is considered possibly his finest book but it was *The Turn of the Screw* (1898), a classic ghost story, that established James as the true exponent of the psychological novel. He became a British subject in 1915 and died the following year, shortly after receiving the Order of Merit. His ashes were interred in the Cambridge Cemetery, Cambridge, Massachusetts.

E.F. Benson 1867–1940

Benson was born into the rarefied, cloistered world of the English public school and the Anglican Church. His father was the first Master of Wellington College, which had been established only nine years before Benson's birth. The family moved to Lincoln in 1873 following Benson senior's appointment as Chancellor. Three years later the Bensons moved again, this time to Cornwall, where Edward Benson became the first Bishop of Truro. Six years later he was appointed Archbishop of Canterbury.

E.F. Benson was educated at Marlborough College in Wiltshire. His blissful childhood and his student days at Cambridge became the subject of several books, including *David Blaize* (1916) and *David of King's* (1924). Benson was a keen sportsman and archaeologist, working on sites in Greece and Egypt. His first novel, *Dodo*, was published in 1893 and became an instant bestseller; *Mammon & Co.* (1899) sold eight thousand copies on the day of publication. He also wrote ghost stories and biographies of Charlotte Brontë, Queen Victoria and Sir Francis Drake – among other subjects. Plagued by arthritis, E.F. Benson died in London of throat cancer in 1940.

BATEMAN'S

'WE HAVE SEEN AN advertisement of her, and we have reached her down an enlarged rabbit-hole of a lane ... We entered and felt her Spirit – Her Feng Shui – to be good. We went through every room and found no shadow of ancient regrets, stifled miseries, nor any malice', Kipling wrote of his beloved home at Burwash in his autobiographical *Something of Myself* (1937).

Built of sandstone by a local ironmaster in 1634, Bateman's was Rudyard Kipling's refuge from the world and it was here that he found peace and contentment. The house lies about twenty-five miles to the north-east of The Elms, Kipling's old home at Rottingdean, near Brighton. His considerable fame proved a hindrance and he took exception to the hoards of sightseers who would descend on The Elms, peering into his garden and even sometimes into the house. Inevitably, but much against his wishes, Kipling had become public property.

The only course of action was to find a house that would afford him total privacy and seclusion. On 23 May 1902 Kipling read in the local newspaper that an imposing Jacobean house he and his American wife Carrie had viewed two years earlier was back on the market, having been let in the interim. 'We have loved it ever since our first sight of it,' he wrote later.

Kipling recalled the original asking price – in excess of £10,000. Using an alias – the name of Smith – he requested an appointment to view and acquired Bateman's, together with an old mill on the river and 33 acres of land, for the sum of £9,300. Alexander Scrimgeour, a stockbroker from whom Kipling bought the house, appeared to be unaware that he was dealing with one of Britain's most eminent writers.

Kipling loved the garden at Bateman's just as much as the house, and he devoted much of his time to designing and landscaping it. He planted yew hedges to provide concealment from prying eyes and he even created a pear arch. Visitors to Bateman's, which has been in the care of the National Trust since 1939, can witness the results of his efforts and they can also take a stroll through the glorious rose garden, which he designed after receiving the Nobel Prize for Literature in Stockholm in 1907. He also gained more land over the years in order to write well away from public scrutiny.

Although Kipling relished his privacy at Bateman's, he liked to socialize. However, in an effort to discourage visitors from outstaying their welcome, he adopted a clever trick. He would invite them to take a stroll with him in the garden and then discreetly lead them past the sundial, which somehow always seemed a little fast. He would then suggest they bid their farewells.

A tour of the house evokes the spirit and character of Rudyard Kipling, especially the book-lined study where the author wrote on a French walnut draw-leaf table, which remains cluttered with pen trays, pins, boxes of paper clips and a paperweight that might have belonged to the colonial administrator and first Governor-General of Bengal, Warren Hastings. Oriental rugs and various Eastern artefacts reflect Kipling's travels throughout the Empire.

The study was Kipling's powerhouse, where he would work uninterrupted for hours. It was in this room that Kipling created

Nestling in a natural bowl under the Sussex Downs, Bateman's was the perfect retreat for a writer. It was in the study upstairs that Kipling found space for his two thousand books.

Puck of Pook's Hill (1906), the hillside view from his window providing the inspiration.

From the moment he took up residence, Bateman's was crucial to Kipling's work, helping to shape and influence his writing. Shielded at last from his devoted fans, and protected by the eternally faithful Carrie, Kipling's imagination was reawakened during those early years. In addition to *Puck of Pook's Hill*, he produced *Traffics and Discoveries* (1904), *Actions and Reactions* (1909) and *Rewards and Fairies* (1910).

A constant stream of visitors passed through the house – writers, publishers and politicians among them. Kipling's cousin, Stanley Baldwin, was a regular caller, although the writer had little respect for the Conservative politician who unexpectedly became Prime Minister in 1923, describing him as 'a socialist at heart'.

In 1914, twelve years after the Kiplings moved to Bateman's, Britain was plunged into war, its effects reaching deep into the heart of the Sussex countryside. Aware that hostilities would have a detrimental influence on trade, Kipling decided the best course of action was to be self-sufficient. He bought forty sheep and also built up a herd of pedigree Guernsey cows to supply the estate with butter and milk. In addition he invested in a herd of red Sussex Shorthorn cattle and grew crops, but with few men available to work the land, Kipling's main concern was the shortage of labour on the estate and its long-term implications, and he remarked that there was only 'one man over age to look after 160 acres of land and 27 cattle'.

The house itself played a vital role in the Great War. In common with many other landowners, Kipling billeted troops at Bateman's, adapting Dudwell Farmhouse into a refuge for shell-shocked and wounded soldiers.

Long before the outbreak of war, Kipling's imagination was captured by the pleasures of motoring. He became an ardent motorist, though he never drove himself and always employed a chauffeur. For him, even a short drive was an adventure and such was his passion for motoring that he regularly dispatched memos to the Automobile Association. He also became something of a motoring journalist, producing articles for the national press.

However, not all his motoring experiences were without incident. When house-hunting the Kiplings travelled by train to view Bateman's as his steam-driven Locomobile had broken down. On show in the grounds of the house is a 1928 Rolls Royce Phantom 1. Kipling chose the Rolls Royce as his preferred mode of transport. 'It was the only car I could afford,' he once remarked dryly.

Bateman's was Kipling's spiritual home and it was here that he found true and complete happiness. He was its master for thirty-four memorable years and it is a tribute to the affection in which he held Bateman's that he once described it as 'a real house in which to settle down for keeps ... a good and peaceable place'.

Rudyard Kipling 1865–1936

Born in Bombay, Kipling was the son of John Lockwood Kipling, Principal of the School of Art in Lahore, and his wife Alice. The couple named their son Rudyard after the Staffordshire lake where they courted in the early 1860s. Kipling was educated at the United Services College at Westward Ho! in Devon before returning to India where he was employed as a journalist. He settled in England in 1889 and his first novel *The Light that Failed* was published the following year. In 1892 he married Caroline (Carrie) sister of the American author and publisher Wolcott Balestier. Collections of verse and short stories followed, and in the mid-1890s he produced the two 'Jungle Books' – classics among animal stories. The semi-autobiographical *Stalky & Co* (1899) was inspired by his schooldays; *Kim* and the *Just So* stories were published in 1901 and 1902 respectively.

The First World War cast a dark cloud over Kipling's life: his only son John was killed in France in 1915.

GROOMBRIDGE PLACE
(Garden access only)

OVER THE YEARS, ingenious plots and a tangible period atmosphere have captured the imagination of millions of fans of the Sherlock Holmes mysteries throughout the world, but it is often the prominent role of the English country house in Conan Doyle's gripping tales that readers find particularly intriguing. In some instances, the author has been influenced by his knowledge of real landmarks: places he has known and visited many times. One prime example of Conan Doyle using somewhere that is real, not imagined, as a crucial setting for one of his stories is Groombridge Place, near Tunbridge Wells.

Conan Doyle lived nearby in Crowborough in East Sussex for the last twenty-three years of his life and visited the house on a number of occasions, sometimes on foot from his home, Windlesham Manor. His daughter Jean recalled him taking house guests to visit Groombridge Place. 'He was fascinated by the old house and felt that by showing it off to visitors from overseas, he was introducing them to the very essence of England,' she wrote. Conan Doyle even admits on the flyleaf of a first edition of the Sherlock Holmes mystery, *The Valley of Fear* (1915), that Groombridge Place is the model for Birlstone Manor in the story.

He describes the setting with remarkable accuracy, indicating how intimately he knew the house and gardens, although he clearly used artistic licence to rewrite Groombridge Place's history and change details of its setting. However, literary scholars have acknowledged that Conan Doyle made little effort to disguise Groombridge Place in *The Valley of Fear*. Elsewhere, the question of identifying country house locations used in the Holmes stories becomes a mystery almost worthy of a Conan Doyle novel.

Described as one of the finest seventeenth-century classical mansions in England, Groombridge Place was built by Philip Packer, Clerk of the Privy Seal to Charles II, to a design partly drawn up by Sir Christopher Wren, a friend of Packer's. John Evelyn was invited to help plan the new leisure gardens.

Groombridge Place has changed little since it was built more than

350 years ago. The stone portico was added and the sash windows replaced lattice casements in the eighteenth century. Bathrooms and power were introduced to the house in the 1920s. The spring-fed moat, for which Groombridge Place is renowned, is the oldest surviving feature, dating from the mid-thirteenth century and containing over an acre of surface water.

Strolling in the grounds highlights the similarities between Groombridge Place and Birlstone Manor. The setting strongly evokes the atmosphere of *The Valley of Fear*. In the story, the house is reached by a drawbridge spanning 'a beautiful broad moat, as still and luminous as quicksilver in the cold winter sunshine'. The drawbridge plays a key role in the tale, though in reality there is no such feature at Groombridge Place.

Conan Doyle begins Chapter 3 of *The Valley of Fear* by moving the action to Sussex and describing Birlstone Manor in a wider context. Employing Dr John Watson in his familiar guise as narrator, he writes:

Dating from around 1230, the moat is the oldest surviving feature at Groombridge Place. The spring-fed moat contains more than an acre of surface water and includes shoals of carp and roach.

The village of Birlstone is a small and very ancient cluster of half-timbered cottages on the northern border of the county of Sussex. It is the centre for a considerable area of country, since Tunbridge Wells, the nearest place of importance, is ten or twelve miles to the eastward, over the borders of Kent. About half a mile from the town, standing in an old park famous for its huge beech trees, is the ancient Manor House of Birlstone. Part of this venerable building dates back to the time of the first crusade, when Hugo de Capus built a fortalice in the centre of the estate....This was destroyed by fire in 1543, and some of its smoke-blackened corner stones were used when, in Jacobean times, a brick country house rose upon the ruins of the feudal castle.

Conan Doyle writes about Birlstone's 'many gables and small diamond-paned windows ... [the house] still much as the builder had left it in the early seventeenth century'. He touches on past rituals and the well-ordered structure of daily life at Birlstone: 'three centuries of births and of homecomings, of country dances and of the meetings of fox hunters.' He also dwells on the aftermath of a murder at Birlstone, the air of menace that suddenly envelops the house:

> Strange that now in its old age this dark business should have cast its shadow upon the venerable walls! And yet those strange, peaked roofs and quaint, overhung gables were a fitting covering to a grim and terrible intrigue. As I [Watson] looked at the deep-set windows and the long sweep of the dull-coloured, water-lapped front, I felt no more fitting scene could be set for such a tragedy.

The gardens at Groombridge were unseen and undiscovered, except for a privileged few, for over three hundred years. They reflect the skill and talent of landscape gardeners and horticulturalists down the centuries, from traditional concepts to contemporary designs. The garden where Watson walks in *The Valley of Fear* has been re-established in recent years. A small museum, dedicated to Sherlock Holmes and Groombridge's influence on his creator, was opened in 1995.

In *The Valley of Fear*, Dr Watson overhears an important conversation between two suspects while walking in the garden at Birlstone Manor. Sir Arthur Conan Doyle confirmed that he modelled the house and its setting on Groombridge Place.

Sir Arthur Conan Doyle 1859–1930

Arthur Conan Doyle was born of Irish parentage in Edinburgh in 1859, the third of nine children. His father was a highly strung artist and draughtsman, given to violent mood swings. Conan Doyle was educated at Stonyhurst College and studied medicine at Edinburgh, where he met his mentor, Joseph Bell. He qualified as a GP and worked in Southsea on the Hampshire coast. Poverty led to writing and it was while he was at Southsea that he created Sherlock Holmes. The most famous detective in literature made his debut in *A Study in Scarlet* (1887). Holmes featured in fifty-six short stories and four novels, spanning a forty-year period. Conan Doyle died three years after the great detective solved his last case.

Sherlock Holmes gave Conan Doyle fame, happiness and financial security, but soon the author became frustrated by the limitations the success of the character imposed on his writing career. He contrived to kill off Holmes but reckoned without his loyal readers. There was an unprecedented outcry over the detective's departure and, at the dawn of the twentieth century, Conan Doyle somewhat reluctantly brought Holmes back to life. In addition to detective fiction, he wrote several historical novels, including *Micah Clarke* (1889), *The White Company* (1891) and the Brigadier Gerard series. *The Lost World* (1912), a science-fiction adventure yarn about an expedition into the deep regions of the Amazon, became one of Conan Doyle's most popular stories. In 1926 he published his *History of Spiritualism*, one of several books he wrote on the subject. He married twice. Conan Doyle was knighted in 1902, following the publication of a pamphlet entitled *The War in South Africa: Its Causes and Conduct*, in which he justified British action. He served as a physician during the Second Boer War.

CHARLESTON FARMHOUSE

IT WAS WHILE WALKING on the South Downs one day in 1916 that Virginia Woolf spotted Charleston Farmhouse, standing in an isolated fold of the Sussex landscape. The moment she saw it she felt instinctively that it would be the perfect rural retreat for her sister, the artist Vanessa Bell. Situated at the foot of Firle Beacon and somewhat austere, especially when seen in the depths of winter, outwardly Charleston is not perhaps the most picturesque of houses, yet it possesses a certain charm and its literary legacy and the ghosts of its long-departed occupants vividly bring the imagination to life.

With the help of the well-versed tour guides, you can picture Virginia Woolf at Charleston, debating philosophy with Vanessa Bell, who apparently was once telephoned there by Picasso. She refused to speak to the legendary painter, who was staying in the area, citing the new-fangled communication system as the reason.

On initial inspection Bell was not over-impressed with the

Originally half-timbered, Charleston Farmhouse lacked today's modern comforts when Vanessa Bell moved here midway through the First World War. In those early days, there was no telephone, electricity or heating system.

sixteenth-century stone farmhouse. However, a second visit several days later persuaded her that the house met her requirements, and those of her expanding family, perfectly, although the tenant farmer who sub-let Charleston to Bell could never have foreseen that one day the farmhouse would achieve international status as the summer retreat of the noted Bloomsbury Group.

Vanessa Bell soon moved to the rickety old farmhouse but it was hardly a conventional household. The ménage included Bell's children, Quentin and Julian, her homosexual lover and fellow artist Duncan Grant, and on occasion her estranged husband Clive, the noted critic and aesthete, who later lived here permanently. Grant's boyfriend, the writer David Garnett, was also part of the group. The two men were pacifists and managed to avoid conscription by gaining employment in the area as farm labourers.

Among the many writers who regularly descended on Charleston were Lytton Strachey and E.M. Forster, the economist Maynard Keynes, who lived in the area and kept a room at the farmhouse for many years, and Virginia Woolf and her husband Leonard, who had a cottage at nearby Rodmell. These literary figures were part of an intellectual, unorthodox community at Charleston whose members did not live by the traditional constraints of the time and where weekends and long summer evenings were spent engaged in intense debate and discussion. At Charleston they were able to create their own hedonistic world, essentially cushioned from the grim reminders of reality.

Charleston 'is really so lovely', enthused Bell in a letter written in the autumn of 1916, 'very solid and simple with flat walls in that lovely mixture of brick and flint that they use about here – and perfectly flat windows in the walls and wonderful tiled roofs'.

The 'Eminent Charlestonians', as they were known, loved this unspoiled corner of the county, savouring, as Bell's son Quentin described it:

> the aesthetic comfort of Sussex gardens full of flowers in which
> plaster-casts from the antique slowly disintegrated from year
> to year; high studios that were also living rooms in which were
> painted decorations of a kind that would now be considered

dreadfully fussy and old-fashioned; rooms made for ease rather than show, on the walls of which hung the spoils of more adventurous years.

A visit to Charleston brings the Bloomsbury world to life. Quirky, idiosyncratic and steeped in character, the farmhouse reflects the spirit, taste and highly individual decorative, post-Impressionist style of those who knew and loved it and made it their home. There is a great deal to see and much to spark the imagination, including the frescoes and the walls onto which Duncan Grant painted directly.

One of Charleston's most enchanting features is the garden room where members of the Bloomsbury Group would relax over a drink, with the doors wide open to allow in the scented air of evening. T.S. Eliot would read extracts from *The Waste Land* (1922), published by the Woolfs at the Hogarth Press, and the iconoclast Lytton Strachey would quote passages from his highly successful,

The walled garden at Charleston was created by Vanessa Bell and Duncan Grant to designs by Roger Fry. Hen runs and vegetable plots were replaced by plants, flowers, mosaic pavements and tile-edged pools.

Vanessa Bell's two sons, Quentin and Julian, sailed a small boat on the pond at Charleston as children. In later life, Quentin used mud from the bottom to mould sculptures, pots and lamps.

ground-breaking work of biography *Eminent Victorians* (1918). Grant would regularly fall asleep.

The Bloomsbury Group's summer commune became a byword for free expression and creative energy at the height of Modernism and, against this heady backdrop, Quentin and Julian Bell established the circle's own newspaper, the *Charleston Bulletin*, in 1923. Although not exactly enamoured of her work as a novelist, Quentin, then aged thirteen, approached his aunt, Virginia Woolf, and invited her to contribute. Woolf jumped at the chance to be associated with the publication and between 1923 and 1927 they worked together on supplements to the *Bulletin*, written or dictated by Woolf and eagerly illustrated by Quentin.

The purpose of the newspaper was to satirize the Bloomsbury Group, its gently irreverent, mocking tone and surreal vignettes appealing in the main to its readers' sense of mischief. No one escaped inclusion. There is even reference to Clive Bell's baldness, suggesting that it might have been caused by the 'indiscriminate application of fresh snowballs to an insufficiently protected pate'.

Charleston Farmhouse continued as an artistic and literary community until Duncan Grant's death in 1978. Today, the house and garden, which are managed by the Charleston Trust, play host to thousands of visitors annually, many of whom are inspired by regular creative workshops, lectures on art and literature and local themed walks.

Perhaps it is best left to one of the younger members of the Bloomsbury Group to convey something of the flavour of daily life here. Quentin Bell, who died in 1996 aged eighty-six, described what it was like to grow up in this extraordinary and incestuous household. 'It was disorderly and might be called disreputable, but the atmosphere was congenial,' he recalled.

The Bloomsbury Group

This distinctly Bohemian circle of influential writers, artists and philosophers originated in London's Bloomsbury, the former home of British publishing where many leading literary luminaries had settled. At its core was Virginia Woolf, one of the Bloomsbury Group's leading lights. Between the wars, the Bloomsbury Group transformed and revolutionized preconceived ideas on relationships and sexual freedom. Though radical, liberated and highly intelligent, its members struggled to find lasting happiness themselves, the complex web of inter-group affairs and sexual liaisons often causing public outrage. However, by the 1960s, the start of a new era of sexual liberation, there was a revival of interest in the Bloomsbury Group, prompting an assortment of biographical studies.

MONK'S HOUSE

To WALK FROM MONK'S HOUSE across the water meadows to the banks of the River Ouse a mile away is to follow in the final steps of Virginia Woolf and one can sense an almost palpable air of sadness in the fields and along the hedgerows of this rural backwater of East Sussex. In March 1941, less than two years after the outbreak of war, Woolf was once more struggling with the demons that had dogged her life for so long – depression and dark despair. She and her husband Leonard had seen their London home bombed the previous year and now she feared the outcome of war and the devastating effects of the dreaded enemy bombers that flew over their beloved cottage.

On 28 March, Woolf decided her fate. She left a note to Leonard which began: 'Dearest, I feel certain I am going mad again ... We can't go through another one of those terrible times.' She walked across the water meadows to the riverbank and, filling her pockets with stones, waded into the water. Jan Morris, in *Travels with*

Virginia Woolf, considered it apt 'that when she came to end her life, she should do so in the water of the English river that ran within sight of her own house, among the Sussex landscapes that she loved: the human spirit immersed at the end in the spirit of place.'

The Woolfs bought Monk's House in July 1919, paying £700 for it at auction in Lewes. Their previous summer home, where they lived until the lease expired, was near the neighbouring village of Beddingham. Woolf loved this corner of Sussex and was particularly struck by the glorious vista of the South Downs from the garden of Monk's House. In 1928 they extended the three-quarter acre plot in order to preserve the view.

Though Monk's House represented a rural idyll, conditions were primitive. In her diary, Woolf describes in some detail the state of the weather-boarded cottage when it was being offered for sale: 'These rooms are small, I said to myself ... The kitchen is distinctly bad. Theres an oil stove & no grate. Nor is there hot water, nor a bath, & as for the E.C. [earth closet] I was never shown it.'

Despite obvious initial doubts, Woolf recognized that Monk's House had great potential. However, it was the garden and the setting that clinched the sale:

> These prudent objections kept excitement at bay; yet even they were forced to yield place to a profound pleasure at the size & shape & fertility & wildness of the garden ... I could fancy a very pleasant walk in the orchard under the apple trees, with the grey extinguisher of the church steeple pointing my boundary ... There is little ceremony or precision at Monks House. It is an unpretending house, long & low, a house of many doors; on one side fronting the street of Rodmell ... though the street of Rodmell is at our end little more than a cart track running out on to the flat of the water meadows.

Soon, and for a while, she was content and the financial rewards of writing allowed the Woolfs to transform Monk's House, altering it and adding to it to suit their requirements. They carried out improvements to the kitchen and installed a hot water range and a bathroom with a water closet. *Mrs Dalloway* paid for much of the

Virginia and Leonard Woolf were happy at Monk's House, though they found the sound of children's shrill voices in the cricket field and the pealing of the church bells next door infuriating and intrusive.

work and, in her diary for 1925, Woolf wrote: 'I'm out to make £300 this summer by writing.' The success of the book enabled the Woolfs to redesign the reception rooms, creating 'our large combined drawing eating room, with its 5 windows, its beams down the middle & flowers and leaves nodding in all round us.'

Orlando funded an extension to the east end of the cottage, which was originally planned as a sitting room but soon became Woolf's bedroom. To reach it necessitated climbing a short flight of outside stairs by the kitchen door. Moody and mercurial, she relished her own space, as well as the freedom and independence of writing.

In addition to her own bedroom, Woolf built a writing room deep in the garden at Monk's House. Here she would often spend up to twelve hours alone, her gaze falling at times on the Ouse Valley and Mount Caburn, the hill rising dramatically above the rooftops of Lewes. She would often look to the South Downs for inspiration, watching them 'turn from green to blue, like opals', in the fading light of evening.

The writing room today includes many fascinating photographs of the Woolfs at Monk's House, some of which depict the couple relaxing with family and friends. It was not uncommon to find a coterie of writers, critics and assorted intellectuals in the garden or in the vicinity of the writing room. T.S. Eliot, E.M. Forster and members of the renowned Bloomsbury Group were among the visitors. Conversation was invariably stimulating and high-spirited.

'Our orchard is the very place to sit and talk for hours in,' Woolf wrote in a letter to Roger Fry, founder of the Omega Workshops, in 1920. 'What I like best is the water meadow onto which our garden opens. You see every down all the way round you.'

Homely and unpretentious, Monk's House is small by National Trust standards. The tour is short, comprising sitting room, dining room, kitchen and bedroom, but it does capture the spirit of this most enigmatic of British novelists. During Woolf's time at Monk's House, the place often swarmed with a variety of very different residents; there was a marmoset, several dogs, a tank of fish and even a swallow that nested in the hall. There were books everywhere, many of them published at the Hogarth Press with covers designed by her sister, Vanessa Bell.

Though initially viewed with scepticism and suspicion by the people of Rodmell, during their years at Monk's House Leonard and Virginia Woolf became established and active members of the community. She became treasurer of the local branch of the Women's Institute and he was appointed a school governor and treasurer of the local cricket club.

Woolf's last book, *Between the Acts* (1941), is in many ways a requiem for Rodmell and the people and places of this part of Sussex. The novel includes the staging of a play at Pointz Hall, an Elizabethan manor inspired by nearby Glynde Place and Firle Place. There is great attention to detail. Woolf even makes reference to the nesting swallows and fishponds found in the garden of Monk's House.

After Woolf's death, it was three weeks before her body was found. The manner of her passing came as no surprise to Leonard. He had lived with and witnessed her torment and deep unhappiness for years. Her ashes were buried in the garden at Monk's House, beneath one of a pair of elm trees that stood a few yards from her cherished writing room and in the shadow of her dearly loved Downs – 'vast, smooth, shaven, serene'.

Following his wife's death, Leonard wrote:

> One must be crucified on one's own private cross.... I know that
> V will not come across the garden ... and yet I look in that direc-
> tion for her. I know that she is drowned and yet I listen for her to
> come in at the door. I know that it is the last page and yet I turn
> it over.'

Leonard outlived his wife by twenty-eight years. His remains lie in
the garden of Monk's House, which passed to the National Trust in
1969.

Virginia Woolf 1882–1941

Born in London, the daughter of Sir Leslie Stephen, founding editor of the
Dictionary of National Biography, Virginia was, from a young age, the chief
storyteller in the family. She was educated at home. She began her literary
career as a biography critic for the *Times Literary Supplement*. In 1912 she
married Leonard Woolf and together, in 1917, they founded the Hogarth Press,
which published some of her best work. Her third novel *Jacob's Room* (1922) is
acknowledged as a turning point in her writing and the development of fiction,
demonstrating her pioneering use of narrative and language. The book raised
her profile and established her as a prominent figure in the Modernist movement.
Subsequent novels, including *Mrs Dalloway* (1925), *To the Lighthouse* (1927)
and *A Room of One's Own* (1929) reflect her stream-of-consciousness style of
writing. Plagued for much of her life by depression and self-doubt, her published
letters and diaries evoke the life and times of a flawed genius.

UPPARK HOUSE

Occupying a superb hilltop setting on the South Downs
of Sussex, Uppark is one of the county's finest country houses.
Wandering through its rooms, gazing at the impressive detail of its
glorious Georgian interior, it is hard to believe that, as recently as
August 1989, as a direct result of a workman's torch setting light
to the roof, Uppark was ravaged by a devastating fire that ripped
through the house, destroying everything in its path. The first floor

was completely gutted. However, thanks to the sterling efforts of firefighters and staff, most of the ground floor contents were saved.

The National Trust, which had acquired Uppark in 1954, faced an agonizing decision. Should the late seventeenth-century house be restored, or left as a ghostly ruin, its charred remains serving as a tragic reminder of Uppark's past glory? Amid much controversy and after lengthy deliberation, a decision was made by the Trust to restore the house to how it was immediately before the fire – as if the dreadful events of that summer's day had never happened. The Trust faced a mammoth task. Eventually the work was completed and Uppark House reopened in 1995.

A century before the fire, Uppark House defined the age – the Victorian era of social divisions, moral complexities and great privilege. Uppark reflected a way of life that has long gone – the days of weekend house parties, servants below stairs and gracious living. The young Herbert George Wells (H.G. Wells) witnessed that world, but as an outsider. Wells was no aristocrat or wealthy landowner.

His father Joseph was employed as a gardener at Uppark, the country seat of the Fetherstonhaughs. His mother Sarah worked at the house as a lady's maid. The couple married in 1853 and later ran a china business. After Wells's birth the couple separated and, in 1880, Sarah returned to Uppark where she was employed as resident housekeeper for the next thirteen years.

Wells was fourteen when his mother began the job and he stayed in the servants' quarters at Uppark while waiting to begin the next stage of his life – working as an apprentice in a chemist's shop in nearby Midhurst, which he later used as the model for Wimblehurst in his novel *Tono-Bungay*.

Arriving at Uppark, the young, impressionable Wells was immediately thrust into a world that was completely foreign to him. He was permitted to borrow books from the great library, which included works by Voltaire and Tom Paine. He was a prodigious reader and this crucial period of learning combined with what he observed all around him at Uppark – the lower ranks deferring to the immensely rich – helped shape and influence his political views. He loved the beauty of Uppark and its sprawling parkland, but he came to resent what it symbolized in the greater world – the widening social divide. He wrote: 'For me at any rate, the house at Uppark was alive and potent. The place had a great effect on me; it retained a vitality that altogether overshadowed the insignificant ebbing trickle of upstairs life.'

In *Tono-Bungay*, Wells describes a grand country house on the North Downs of Kent. While it is the work of his imagination, the house, Bladesover, is modelled on Uppark. He denied, however, that the housekeeper in the story was based on his mother. His time at Uppark would also prove useful when he wrote *The Time Machine*, his vision of a two-tier society in the distant future. The ventilation shafts in this book connect the upper and lower domains of two species, the Eloi – the ruling classes – and the Morlocks – ape-like humanoids who live in darkness underground and surface only at night.

Linking the dairy, stables, restaurant and shop, the early nineteenth-century ventilation system at Uppark is strikingly similar. Wells's memory of this dank, dark warren of shafts, tunnels and passages might well have inspired him to create the Morlocks' strange, subterranean world. His dislike of the hierarchical, upstairs-downstairs structure of society in the closing stages of the Victorian era is without question.

H.G. Wells 1866–1946

Born in Bromley, Kent, H.G. Wells attended school at Midhurst in West Sussex, later writing, 'I found something very agreeable and picturesque in its clean and cobbled streets, its odd turnings and abrupt corners, and in the pleasant park that crowds up one side of the town.' Wells won a scholarship to the Normal School of Science in South Kensington and studied biology, obtaining a BSc in 1890. The success of his short stories led to a career as a full-time writer. Wells had a tremendous zest for life, throwing himself into his work and taking a keen interest in contemporary issues. Among his many books are *Kipps* (1905) and *The History of Mr Polly* (1910), although he established his name with the publication of *The Time Machine* (1895). Acknowledged as a unique writing talent and a exceptional visionary, he became a prominent pioneer in the genre of science-fiction.

LONDON

KEATS HOUSE

HAMPSTEAD HAS EXPANDED SIGNIFICANTLY since the poet John Keats made his home at Wentworth Place, now known as Keats House, in the early years of the nineteenth century. Not only has this most charming and picturesque of London villages changed dramatically in the two hundred or so years since the poet lived here, but his reputation and influence are reflected in its leafy streets and thoroughfares. Keats House is located in Keats Grove and a couple of streets away can be found The Keats Group Practice, which seems appropriate given that Keats was apprenticed to a surgeon and was later a medical student in the London hospitals.

Keats House in Hampstead has been restored in the style of the early nineteenth century. The garden is stocked with fruit trees, plants and shrubs in keeping with the Regency period.

It is all a far cry from the brief period when Keats lived here. Then, he was struggling and virtually unknown, his reputation yet to be made, his future as a poet uncertain. Wentworth Place was almost new when Keats moved here; the Regency villa was divided into two units but designed to appear as one house. Keats first visited Wentworth Place in 1817. Charles Brown, a bachelor, then occupied the house, living in the eastern part; the larger, western part was the home of Charles Wentworth Dilke and his wife and family.

Keats first moved to lodgings in nearby Well Walk, to be near the poet and editor Leigh Hunt, whom he greatly admired. Among Hunt's circle were Shelley and the painter Benjamin Haydon. Keats became friends with Brown and Wentworth Dilke, whose literary aspirations, it seems, brought them into contact with Hunt.

Keats's friendship with Brown, a talented amateur artist, was a particularly close one and the two men embarked on a walking tour of Scotland. When Keats's brother Tom died in 1818, Brown invited him to share his part of Wentworth Place. His monthly rent was £5 (about £250 today), plus half the liquor bill. Keats had always been peripatetic, residing at countless different addresses in different parts of London. Unlike his previous lodgings, the move to Wentworth Place afforded Keats a sense of comfort and contentment.

He knew the occupants and was encouraged to become part of their circle; the place represented a small, secure community. He also had the use of the entire garden, which was a bonus. Although he didn't own the house, he felt at home there; it brought out the best in him. At Wentworth Place, Keats was conveniently close to many of his literary friends and associates. He was also within relatively easy reach of his publisher, John Taylor, in the city.

Keats's life changed immeasurably in the spring of 1819 when Mrs Brawne, a widow, and her three children moved in next door, following the departure of the Dilkes family. Eighteen-year-old Fanny, the eldest of the children, captured Keats's heart almost from the moment he met her. He fell deeply and hopelessly in love with her, though Fanny was not (in that era) of age. There were other hurdles too. Keats had no prospects: his two books of poetry had not sold well and he was attacked in the press for his association with Leigh Hunt's circle, whose members were largely radical and anti-government.

Keats's instinct was to banish Fanny Brawne from his life. However, his deep feelings and romantic obsession for Fanny made it impossible to distance himself from her. He was especially productive in the spring of 1819, producing six outstanding odes, including the famous 'Ode to a Nightingale', and much other material during this period, and it was later acknowledged, not surprisingly, that Keats's deep-rooted feelings for Fanny prompted this astonishing outpouring of poetry. In short, she was his muse. The couple become engaged and exchanged rings, although they did not marry.

When Keats became ill with tuberculosis, albeit in its early stages, in February 1820, he was forbidden from seeing Fanny, though their love endured and they regularly exchanged letters. Keats moved to Kentish Town at one point during the illness that would eventually kill him, but returned to Wentworth Place and was at this stage nursed by Fanny. By now, Brown had vacated his part of the house, allowing Keats full use of it. After Keats departed for Italy in September 1820, in the fervent hope that the Mediterranean climate would prolong his life, Fanny and her mother continued to reside at Wentworth Place until 1830. Keats's sister, also called Fanny, and her husband came to live in Brown's share of the house.

In 1838 Wentworth Place became the property of Eliza Jane Chester, a retired actress and a favourite of George IV, who converted the two units into one house and added a large room for entertaining onto one end of it. In

A bust of Keats by the American sculptor and poet Anne Whitney. Still only a young man, the terrible, insidious effects of tuberculosis reduced Keats to a shadow of his former self.

subsequent years the house passed into the hands of a succession of owners; in 1895 a plaque was unveiled to mark Keats's centenary and eventually a charity was formed to protect the house for the nation. Incredibly, in 1920, Wentworth Place was threatened with demolition before finally opening to the public as the Keats Memorial House in May 1925.

During his fourteen months at Wentworth Place, Keats occupied much of his time by reading and writing; he would often spend long periods of his day indolently in bed. His parlour, which can be viewed, includes bookcases lined with publications Keats is known to have read or owned. Having written 'Ode to a Nightingale' in the garden, Keats placed the manuscript behind a row of books in one of the cases, from where Charles Brown subsequently retrieved it. Also on display in the parlour is Keats's treasured print of

Shakespeare, given to him by his landlady on a visit to the Isle of Wight.

Only two years before he died, while living at Wentworth Place, John Keats experienced a brief period of utter joy and contentment. His overwhelming love for Fanny Brawne gave him a renewed zest for life, driving the creative forces within him as never before. This overwhelmingly happy period in his life became the subject of a film, *Bright Star*, made in 2009. For Keats, sadly, his star burned all too soon.

Over the fireplace in Keats's parlour is a copy of a portrait of the writer seated in this room. The original painting by Joseph Severn hangs in the National Portrait Gallery.

John Keats 1795–1821

Born in London, Keats was the son of the keeper of a livery stable who died when John was eight. He was educated at Enfield and apprenticed to an apothecary surgeon before becoming a medical student at Guy's Hospital, a career path he later abandoned in favour of writing poetry. His initial sonnets were published in *The Examiner* in 1816 and his first volume of poetry appeared the following year. In the subsequent two years Keats produced an impressive volume of work, including his mythological poem 'Endymion' (1818) and 'Ode to a Nightingale' (1819). He died of tuberculosis in Rome, cared for by his artist friend Joseph Severn.

DR JOHNSON'S HOUSE

HEMMED IN BY MODERN office buildings and hidden in a rabbit warren of courts and quaint passages in the heart of the City of London lies a traditional 300-year-old William and Mary town house that became the home of one of Britain's most respected and influential writers. Thomas Carlyle described it as 'a stout, old-fashioned, oak-balustraded house'.

Built by wool merchant Richard Gough around 1700 and the subject of bomb damage during the Blitz, the four-storey house is a rare example of a house of the period to be found within the Square Mile and is the only one of Johnson's eighteen residences in the city to survive. The writer's annual rent was £30. The tiny garden at Gough Square caught the attention of Carlyle who referred to it as 'somewhat larger than a bed-quilt'.

Samuel Johnson lived at this house – 17 Gough Square, a small L-shaped court close to Fleet Street – between 1747 and 1759, spending much of his time there compiling the 41,000 entries for the *Dictionary of the English Language*, published in 1755. Two first editions can be seen in the grey-panelled rooms of the house. The attic where Johnson worked on the dictionary, his assistants standing at a high table like draughtsmen, can also be viewed.

A year before Johnson moved to Gough Square he had been commissioned to write the dictionary that would make his name, but he would pay a heavy price for the chance. The work took nearly ten years and during that time Johnson was often penniless and in poor health.

The house, however, was perfect for his requirements; it allowed him space to work and was close to his printer, William Strahan, who became the lexicographer's first biographer. However, Johnson was constantly in debt and on more than one occasion was threatened with arrest by bailiffs who, at that time, had the power and authority to send a debtor straight to gaol.

During one particularly difficult period of attempting to make ends meet and pay his creditors, Johnson found he owed so much to his milkman that the tradesman tried to have him arrested. The writer responded by using his bed to barricade the front door, yelling through it that he would 'defend his citadel to the utmost'.

During his time at 17 Gough Square, Samuel Johnson was virtually destitute and often unhappy. Originally owned by a city merchant named Gough, the house suffered bomb damage during the Second World War.

Outside the house, near the main entrance, is a blue plaque unveiled by the Royal Society of Arts in 1876. Inside is the parlour into which visitors would have been ushered on arrival. In those earlier days, the ground floor of the house would not have been conducive to entertaining. London's smoggy atmosphere, the effects of coal fires, the constant clip-clop of horses and the lack of proper sanitation in the surrounding streets and squares would have resulted in these rooms becoming dirty, dingy and smelly. Just a few yards from the house, Fleet Street, one of London's busiest thoroughfares, thronged with wig-makers, mercers, snuff dealers and prostitutes.

A pine staircase leads up to the withdrawing room, to which ladies retired after dinner. The first floor of the house was also where Johnson entertained his wide circle of friends, including politicians, actors and members of the clergy. His reputation as an acclaimed writer and his natural sociability qualified him as a popular host whose company was constantly sought.

However, there was another, more poignant reason for Johnson craving the company of others. His beloved wife Tetty died at Gough Square in 1752 and, following her death, Johnson developed a pathological fear of being alone. In the belief that he would go mad if left to his own company, he surrounded himself with as many people as he could find. The house came to witness a constant stream of casual acquaintances, lodgers and distant relatives. Seven years after Tetty's death Johnson moved to smaller lodgings a short distance away in Staple Inn.

In the years after Johnson's death the house had a varied history. During the nineteenth century it was a hotel, a print shop and a storehouse. In 1911, 17 Gough Square was bought by Cecil Harmsworth, brother of the famous newspaper magnates, who said later: 'At the time of my purchase of the house ... it presented every appearance of squalor and decay – it is doubtful whether in the whole of London there existed a more forlorn or dilapidated tenement.' Harmsworth set about restoring Johnson's former home and eventually opened it to the public in 1914. It now operates as a charitable trust.

Samuel Johnson 1709–84

Educated at Lichfield Grammar School, where he developed his well-chronicled love of the English language and Latin and Greek literature, Samuel Johnson became a student of Pembroke College, Oxford, thanks to a small legacy. He suffered bouts of stress and depression and financial difficulties led him to leave Oxford without a degree, although the University awarded him an MA in 1755 and he later received honorary doctorates from Oxford and Trinity College, Dublin. Johnson taught briefly at Market Bosworth before moving to Birmingham, contributing essays to a local newspaper. In 1735 he married Elizabeth Porter, a widow who was twenty years his senior, and the same year they established a private school at Edial, near Lichfield. The enterprise was not a success. In 1737 Johnson left the Midlands for London in the company of David Garrick, the actor, who had been one of his pupils. Johnson's wife later joined him. He wrote parliamentary reports for Edward Cave's *Gentleman's Magazine*, as well as essays, poems and biographies.

In 1747 Johnson was commissioned to compile a new authoritative dictionary illustrated by quotations. Although the *Dictionary of the English Language* cemented his reputation as one of the leading figures of English literature, he continued to be plagued by financial concerns and the spectre of debt. In 1750 he established the twice-weekly *Rambler*, a periodical consisting of moral essays written anonymously by Johnson. His novel *Rasselas* (1759) was completed in seven days. In 1763 he met his biographer James Boswell. Johnson wrote: 'I lately took my friend Boswell and showed him genuine civilized life in an English provincial town. I turned him loose at Lichfield.'

CHARLES DICKENS MUSEUM

Less than three months after an emerging young writer of twenty-five acquired his first family home, an eighteen-year-old princess became queen. Her reign would last over sixty years.

Charles Dickens and his wife, Catherine, moved to 48 Doughty Street, Bloomsbury, on the last day of March 1837, just a year after they married. With them went his young son Charley, his brother Fred and his teenage sister-in-law Mary. Dickens later described the house, which he took on a three-year lease at £80 a year, as 'a frightfully first-class family mansion, involving awful responsibilities'.

With twelve rooms on three storeys, a basement and attics, the solidly built house in Doughty Street afforded Dickens comfort and security commensurate with his new social status as a celebrated writer.

Number 48 is the only one of the fifteen different properties lived in by Dickens and his family that remains intact.

The terraced house in Doughty Street was a mark of Dickens's early success. It was a sizeable property with twelve decent-sized rooms arranged on three storeys. There were also a basement, an attic and a small rear garden. The house was also relatively new, having been built only thirty years earlier. Doughty Street was located in a select district with gates and liveried gatekeepers to deter the less welcome elements of society. The concept of exclusive, gated communities, it seems, is nothing new.

Still newly married, Dickens and Catherine were settled. His time at Doughty Street was blissful. Fascinated by interior decoration, Dickens chose the furniture and wallpaper designs for Doughty Street. The Morning Room was mainly the preserve of Catherine and the children. She spent much of her time on correspondence, while Dickens busied himself in his study. During his two years at Doughty Street, Dickens was typically passionate and productive.

He worked on the final chapters of *Pickwick Papers* and wrote *Nicholas Nickleby* and *Oliver Twist* while here.

He was a disciplined, methodical writer and his day followed a rigid routine. He would write between breakfast and lunch and then, in the afternoon, he would visit his club or take a long walk. These regular perambulations proved invaluable, Dickens drawing inspiration from much of what he witnessed around him. He was a great observer and the appalling scenes of degradation and suffering he saw on his travels through the London streets invariably translated to the page. His frenzied, whirring imagination never ceased. On occasion he worked long into the night at Doughty Street, writing in his study by candlelight. The flickering flames and their dancing reflection fascinated him. 'A ruddy, homely, brilliant glow,' he wrote.

The Dickens family residence was a busy household filled with servants and visitors and the dominating, irresistible presence of the great man whose future literary success already seemed assured. The dining room and the drawing room were the focal point of social activity at Doughty Street. The latter was where Dickens would entertain his guests with amateur theatricals and readings from his books, using his skills as a performer and storyteller to bring his characters to life, while the former was where he would preside over dinner parties, often in the stimulating company of leading writers and actors of the day, among them John Forster, his friend and biographer. An invitation to the court of Charles Dickens was highly sought.

Given Dickens's caring, sympathetic nature and concern for the less privileged, it should come as no surprise to find that servants feature frequently in his books. His sympathetic portrayal of household staff won him praise and support, not least from servants themselves throughout the land.

The kitchen quarters at Doughty Street suggest the working conditions in the house in the middle years of the nineteenth century. In constant demand to deal with the household laundry, the washhouse copper would also have been used annually to boil the Christmas pudding, a tradition Dickens later replicated in his writing. He refers to 'the pudding singing in the copper' in *A Christmas Carol*. Later,

Mrs Cratchit 'left the room alone – too nervous to bear witnesses – to take the pudding up and bring it in.'

It was while at Doughty Street that Catherine gave birth to two daughters, Mary and Katey. However, as well as overwhelming happiness there was tragic loss. Catherine's younger sister, Mary Hogarth, died at Doughty Street aged only seventeen. Dickens felt her passing keenly – 'young, beautiful and good' was the epitaph he composed for her headstone in Kensal Green Cemetery; 'the dearest friend I ever had', he wrote in one of many heart-rending letters following her death. Mary's premature demise led Dickens to suspend work on *Pickwick Papers* and *Oliver Twist* for a month.

After two years, the growing Dickens family moved to Devonshire Terrace in Regent's Park. The house has since been demolished. The Dickens Fellowship bought 48 Doughty Street in 1924 following a campaign to save it from demolition. Number 49 was acquired at the same time. Dickens's former home was officially opened as a museum a year later.

Occasional changes and improvements were made to the house in the subsequent decades. However, the greatest transformation took place in 2012, the year of Dickens's bicentenary. The drawing room had already been restored to its original Regency appearance before innovative conservation techniques and new practices allowed the latest improvements to take place. A tour of the house more than 170 years after Dickens resided there reveals items of original Victorian furniture and an assortment of letters, manuscripts and first editions. The annotated books he used for public performances and lecture tours are also on display.

CARLYLE'S HOUSE

'CHELSEA IS AN UNFASHIONABLE place, that is the secret of it,' the Victorian writer Thomas Carlyle wrote to his wife, Jane, in 1834. In June that year the couple moved to number 5 Cheyne Row (now 24), in that same district of London, renting an early eighteenth-century, Queen Anne terraced house just a stone's throw from the river for £38 per year.

It seems inconceivable, nearly two hundred years later, that what is now one of the capital's most expensive and desirable villages was once so unappealing. 'Chelsea is cheapest of all,' wrote Carlyle, 'A singular heterogeneous kind of spot; very dirty and confused in some places, quite beautiful in others, abounding in antiquities and the traces of great men – Sir Thomas More, Smollett ...'

Carlyle's descriptions of Chelsea and the view of London from the house are fascinating:

> We lie safe down in a little bend in the river away from all the great roads; and have an outlook from the back window to mere leafy regions with here and there a high-peaked old roof looking through. We see nothing of London except by day the summits of St Paul's Cathedral and Westminster Abbey and by night the great Babylon affronting the peaceful skies.

He described nearby Cheyne Walk, a fashionable London address beloved of the literati, as 'a beautiful parade running along the shore of the river, with shops, shady trees, boats lying moored and the smell of shipping and tar'.

The Carlyles moved to London from their home in Scotland in order that Thomas could be at the heart of the literary world, close to editors, publishers and fellow writers. He believed that relocating to the capital would increase his chances of success as an author. He was not rich and the rent on Cheyne Row was affordable.

Inside, the house is arranged on five floors, with a sitting room, or parlour – often used by Carlyle as a study – back dining room, hall and china closet on the ground floor. The interior is authentic Victorian and, reputedly, much as the couple left it. Through the efforts of Carlyle devotees, the house includes many items of furniture that date back to the family's time here.

A tour of 24 Cheyne Row reveals the pattern of daily life in the Carlyle household where the 'Sage of Chelsea', as he was known, entertained and inspired a host of artists, scientists and politicians, as well as many distinguished writer friends and followers – among them Eliot, Ruskin, Tennyson and Dickens. Jane's piano is also on show, played in the house by Frederick Chopin in 1848.

Following a visit to Carlyle's home with her husband Robert, Elizabeth Barrett Browning wrote: 'We have passed an evening with Carlyle; he is one of the most interesting men I can imagine, one of the great sights in England to my mind. I am a Carlyle adorer.'

An American friend, Ellen Twistleton, wrote: 'The Carlyles are both overflowing with intelligence and stores of agreeable conversation. They live in Chelsea, in the most ordinary style imaginable and the most wretched neighbourhood. They had a wonderful effect upon my sensations after passing so many days among well-bred, inoffensive, negative people to come into such an atmosphere.'

The Carlyles spent much of their time engaged in correspondence, writing several thousand letters to each other, to family and to friends, including Dickens and Robert Browning. The correspondence serves as a fascinating social record of the time, offering an absorbing insight into the day-to-day routine at Cheyne Row. Jane's letters are particularly revealing and entertaining. Dickens wrote: 'None of the other writing women come near her at all.'

After the peace and tranquillity of his native Dumfriesshire, Thomas Carlyle found living in London noisy and distracting. He decided to build a sound-proof study at the house in Cheyne Row. 'All the cocks in nature may crow round it, without my hearing a whisper of them!' declared Carlyle, confidently.

Carlyle's attic or garret study at the top of the house draws many visitors. This 20 ft-square room, lit by an overhead skylight and 'artfully ventilated', was completed in 1854 as an additional top storey to the house and built by an engineer he knew from Liverpool, whose services were required to make the room soundproof. Double walls were constructed at the front and back to hide the increasing sound of London traffic and other intrusions, but unfortunately the project was rendered a failure. The architect hadn't taken account of the skylight, which allowed the sound of church bells, steamer sirens and railway whistles to drift in on the breeze.

Jane wrote: 'The silent room is the noisiest in the house and Mr C is very much out of sorts.' Despite the constant interruptions, it was here that Carlyle completed his last great work, a weighty biography of Frederick the Great. It took thirteen years to complete. When it was finished, and no doubt partly in response to Jane's sudden and unexpected death from a heart attack in 1866, Carlyle abandoned the specially designed study, which later became a maid's bedroom.

Thirty years before Jane's untimely passing, one afternoon in 1836 while he was having tea at Cheyne Row, Carlyle received a sudden, shattering piece of news of a very different kind. His friend John Stuart Mill, the philosopher and reformer, rushed into the room to inform the writer that the manuscript for Carlyle's *The History of the French Revolution*, which he had loaned to Mill, had been destroyed. A maidservant had apparently used it to light the fire, believing it to be scrap paper.

It was a fearful blow, dreaded by all writers – the loss of an invaluable piece of work that had taken many precious hours of labour and demanded intense concentration to create. The 171 pages had been 'irrevocably annihilated' wailed a distraught Carlyle. However, he was in a forgiving mood. 'Mill, poor fellow, is very miserable; we must try and keep from him how serious is the loss. It shall be written again.' Carlyle did indeed write it again and the book was published to great acclaim in 1837. A fragment of the ill-fated original manuscript can be seen at Cheyne Row.

Among the many artefacts, letters and documents to be found at the house is a fascinating letter to Carlyle from Benjamin Disraeli, who believed he should be rewarded for inspiring so many writers and literary scholars over the years, and for the impact he had made on Victorian society. It reads:

It is not well that in the sunset of your life you should be disturbed by common cares. I see no reason why a great author should not receive from the nation a pension, as well as a lawyer or a statesman. Unfortunately, the personal power of Her Majesty in this respect is limited. But still it is in the Queen's capacity to settle on an individual an amount equal to a good fellowship as was cheerfully accepted and enjoyed by the great spirit of Johnson and the pure integrity of Southey.'

Carlyle politely declined the offer.

The garden at the rear of the house is also open to visitors, although the view of 'mere leafy regions' is no longer recognizable. In perfect working order is the little privy, which many of Carlyle's guests, including Dickens, would have used over the years.

Still the same size and shape as it was in the 1850s, the garden is a delight, characterized by many colourful plants and shrubs, including Virginia creeper, foxgloves, jasmine, lilac and roses, and noted for its fig tree. Known for his glum, pessimistic view of the world, it was to the garden at Cheyne Row that Carlyle would invariably retreat, wearing his dressing gown and straw hat and smoking his pipe. During interludes spent away from his desk, Carlyle could regularly be found scrubbing the back door flagstone step. He greatly enjoyed the task, apparently finding it a perfect alternative to writing.

In 1885, the artist Benjamin Creswick sculpted a medallion portrait of Thomas Carlyle, which was subsequently placed at the centre of a decorative panel and positioned on the front wall of the writer's former home.

Fourteen years after Thomas Carlyle's death, 24 Cheyne Row became the first writer's house in London to open its doors as a literary shrine. It was acquired through public subscription and among the contributors were the Rt. Hon. Herbert Gladstone, who gave one guinea and Henry James who donated £5. Canon Hardwicke Rawnsley, one of the three founders of the National Trust, also provided funds. The house was given to the Trust in 1936.

Thomas Carlyle 1795–1881

The son of a stonemason, Carlyle was born at Ecclefechan in Dumfriesshire. He was educated at Edinburgh University before entering the teaching profession. He taught for a while in Annan and Kirkcaldy. Carlyle returned to Edinburgh in 1818 to study law, but soon became preoccupied with the theme of German literature. His translation of Goethe's *Wilhelm Meister* in 1824 brought him to the attention of London's influential literary circle. In 1826 he married Jane Welsh and, after two years spent living in Edinburgh, the couple moved to her farm at Craigenputtock, near Dumfries, before settling permanently in London. *Sartor Resartus*, his first major work on social philosophy, was published in instalments in *Fraser's Magazine* (1833–4).

CENTRAL SOUTHERN ENGLAND

THE OLD RECTORY

(Garden access only)

EVELYN WAUGH DESCRIBED IT as 'dark, dank and miserable', but as houses go, the Old Rectory at Farnborough is rather special. It even boasts the highest bathroom in Berkshire, standing 700 feet above sea level, its fittings unchanged since it was used by its most famous resident, John Betjeman, and his family in the years immediately following the Second World War.

It was Betjeman's father-in-law, Field Marshal Lord Chetwode, who bought the Old Rectory at auction in May 1945, as Britain celebrated victory in Europe. He paid £5,100 for the house, which dates from the middle of the eighteenth century and which, until the end of the Second World War, had been occupied by generations of the same clerical family, giving it to the couple as a belated wedding present. They had married twelve years earlier.

Betjeman's wife, Penelope, later wrote to a friend:

> Father has bought us a beautiful William and Mary house 700 feet up on the downs above Wantage, with 12 acres of land, including a wood and two fields. It is a dream of beauty but has no water, no light and is falling down and needs six servants, so it will probably kill us in the end.

In her childhood memoir *The Dangerous Edge of Things*, Betjeman's daughter, the writer Candida Lycett Green, recalls water being pumped up manually from a well: 'Once the water had been pumped, a small trickle came out of the taps in the brown-lino-floored bathroom at the top of the house. Ours and the three farmhouses were the only ones to have running water.' Set against a background of post-war austerity, Candida and her elder brother Paul endured a bleak but contented existence as children at Farnborough, heavy snow and, by today's standards, a frugal life-style leaving a lasting impression on them.

Evelyn Waugh, a friend and contemporary of Betjeman, stayed at the Old Rectory on a number of occasions. After his first visit he told Nancy Mitford that the house 'smelled like a village shop – oil, cheese, bacon, washing'. His diary entry for 31 October 1946 recalls that he went 'to stay with the Betjemans in a lightless, stuffy, cold, poky rectory among beech trees overlooking Wantage. Harness everywhere. A fine collection of nineteenth-century illus-trated books. Delicious food cooked by Penelope. I brought sherry, burgundy, port.'

The Betjemans had been desperate to make the Old Rectory their home. The poet likened the process of securing the house to

John Betjeman described the Old Rectory at Farnborough as 'dirty, but classy looking inside' when he first viewed it in 1945. Architectural historians generally regard it as a quite exceptional house in a sublime setting high on the downs.

'buying a Cezanne, a beautiful picture'. At Farnborough he would have a library for his vast collection of antiquarian books, which, by the end of his life, amounted to 5,000 volumes. More than anything, Betjeman relished the idea of moving to a 'gentleman's house'. During his time at the Old Rectory, Betjeman was typically productive. In 1948 his *Selected Poems* won the Heinemann Award for Literature and, among many other works, he completed *Murray's Architectural Guide for Berkshire* (1949). The Old Rectory was home for six years. But John Betjeman's time there was not entirely without pain or heartache. The house proved to be a constant financial burden and in later years he would come to associate the place with the first serious rift in what became a troubled marriage. The Betjemans sold the house for £11,000 in 1951, moving to nearby Wantage, where Penelope opened a tearoom.

Over the years the Old Rectory's classically English design and handsome south-facing façade have drawn interest from architectural historians and Betjeman enthusiasts, and hardly a day passes when there are not admiring glances from passing motorists and ramblers. The house, which won England's prestigious Finest Parsonage Award in 2008 and lies in Ridgeway country, close to the border of Berkshire and Oxfordshire, is clearly visible from the road.

Dating back to 1749, the Old Rectory has a central bellcote that was added ninety years after the house was built. The idea behind the bell was to summon local children to the village school, housed at that time in the Old Rectory. During his time there, Betjeman rang the bell every year on his son's birthday.

Candida Lycett Green's memory of the bell and its setting is clear:

Our red-brick rectory stood well back from the road, towering beech trees sheltering its east side and a wide lawn before it. A bell hung under a swooping arch on top of the house. It was rung by pulling a thin chain which ran down through two floors into the hall below. On a still day its shrill ting carried over fields and woods for a mile or more and my mum would ring it to summon us for meals.

The present owners of the Old Rectory, Mr and Mrs Michael Todhunter, moved to the house in 1964. Essentially it has remained the same since they bought it, although they added a small dressing room extension and altered the reception hall with the help of interior designer Douglas Clark. Their predecessor, Pat Lawrence, made more significant changes to the house, creating a striking domed drawing room to its east side. The Todhunters have also maintained the famous bell-ringing tradition established by Betjeman.

The stained glass in the west window of the tower of Farnborough's parish church of All Saints depicts symbols of the Resurrection. The window, a memorial to Betjeman, is a blaze of colour in the evening light.

Directly opposite the Old Rectory is the parish church of All Saints, which can be reached from the house via a delightful wooded path running through the 14-acre grounds to the road. One of the church's most striking features is its Betjeman memorial window designed by John Piper.

After the move to Wantage, John Betjeman's spirit seemed to linger at the Old Rectory. He returned there on occasion and recounted the move to Farnborough from the family's previous home at Uffington in Oxfordshire in his only children's book, *Archie and the Strict Baptists* (1977). His time in the village was relatively short but the house held many memories for him, fuelling his imagination.

John Betjeman 1906–84

Born in Highgate, North London, John Betjeman was the son of a furniture manufacturer whose family name was of Dutch origin. Betjeman's talent for poetry and prose was evident even as a child and his study of Victorian architecture while still at school led to a revival of interest in buildings from that period. One of his masters at junior school was T.S. Eliot. Betjeman was further educated at Marlborough and Magdalen College, Oxford. One of his earliest jobs was as a preparatory schoolmaster at Thorpe House School in Gerrards Cross, Buckinghamshire.

During the 1930s Betjeman co-edited the much-loved series of Shell Guides to English Counties before spending the Second World War as a press attaché in Dublin. The early period of his life is highlighted in his blank-verse autobiography *Summoned by Bells* (1960). Collections of verse include *New Bats in Old Belfries* (1945) and *A Few Late Chrysanthemums* (1954). He was knighted in 1969 and became Poet Laureate in 1972.

With his infectious laugh, startled expression and mischievous sense of fun, John Betjeman was a natural performer, his skills and talent highly suited to the medium of television. His quirky, hapless style and endearing air of eccentricity manifested themselves during his time at Farnborough, too. According to the Todhunters, Betjeman was known to reverse his car out of the garage with the doors still closed.

THE KILNS

PICTURING THE FORMER HOME of C.S. Lewis as it was during the middle years of the twentieth century requires a strong imagination. When Lewis first set eyes on The Kilns in July 1930 the setting was essentially rural. Lewis's brother, Warren (Warnie), who also lived at The Kilns, wrote in his diary: 'The house stands at the entrance to its own grounds at the northern foot of Shotover at the end of a narrow lane, which in turn opens off a very bad and little-used road, giving as great privacy as can reasonably be for near a large town.'

Shotover, once a royal hunting forest, remains green and leafy but the rough lanes leading to The Kilns have long been upgraded to serve encroaching post-war housing estates and residential development. The 'large town' to which Warnie refers is, in fact, the city of Oxford, a short distance to the west, on the far side of the ring road.

Warnie describes in his diary the day he and his brother, known to all as Jack, first saw The Kilns from the outside: 'Jack and I went out and saw the place, and I instantly caught the infection. We did not go inside the house, but the eight-acre garden is such stuff as dreams are made on. I never imagined that for us any such garden would ever come within the sphere of discussion.' He refers also to the two brick kilns, which stood to the left of the house and gave it its name. They were in a ruinous state by the time Lewis moved there. In front of the house were a lawn, a tennis court and a bathing pool. Warnie wrote: 'After that a steep wilderness broken with ravines and nooks of all kinds runs up to a little cliff topped by a thistly meadow and then the property ends in a thick belt of fir trees, almost a wood. The view from the cliff over the dim blue distance is simply glorious.'

C.S. Lewis paid £3,300 for the house, which was built in 1922 and therefore relatively new at the time he bought it. Life was never dull during Lewis's subsequent three decades at The Kilns, though the domestic arrangements were unconventional, even by today's standards. Jack and Warnie were joint owners of The Kilns, together with a third party – Mrs Janie Moore, with whom Jack had lodged when he was an undergraduate. Twenty-six years Lewis's senior, Mrs Moore was the mother of Francis 'Paddy' Moore, Lewis's

WWW.CSLEWIS.ORG

When C.S. Lewis saw The Kilns for the first time in the summer of 1930, its immediate surroundings were very different. Nearby were several derelict brick kilns, which he later used for storing coal.

roommate at Keble College, where the two young men were billeted in 1917. Lewis made Mrs Moore a promise, that in the event of his friend's death in the First World War, he would look after both his mother and sister Maureen. Paddy was killed in battle in 1918. Typically, Lewis honoured his pledge and Mrs Moore and her daughter became residents at The Kilns.

Referring to each other as mother and son, Lewis's relationship with Mrs Moore was clearly ambiguous and possibly based on maternal affection and romantic love, but her presence in his life lent it structure and stability. They did not sleep together but had adjoining rooms. Lewis's bedroom, at one end of the house, could only be reached internally through Mrs Moore's room and, perhaps out of an instinctive sense of propriety, he entered and left his bedroom via an outside staircase. Soon Lewis and the others settled into a cosy routine at The Kilns, though there was friction between Mrs Moore and Warnie, who was an alcoholic.

Lewis divided his time between the house and Magdalen College where he had rooms in New Buildings, overlooking glorious parkland dotted with deer. He relished his quite separate life at Magdalen, where he had been elected a fellow and tutor in 1925, although he also lived happily at The Kilns, spending much of his

During Lewis's tenure, The Kilns rang ceaselessly with the sound of conversation and laughter. The writer J.R.R. Tolkien, a friend and contemporary of Lewis, was a frequent visitor.

spare time there. The house brimmed with fun and laughter and there was a constant stream of visitors. There were also lively discussions and debates about books and literature, while in one of the upstairs rooms Maureen played the violin.

During the Second World War, child evacuees came to stay at The Kilns. With Europe in the grip of turmoil once again, an air of gloom pervaded Britain. The future was uncertain and everyone sensed it. Encouraged by the evacuees, Lewis began to write them a story about four children who have to leave London suddenly as a result of enemy bombing. They go to stay with an elderly professor who lives alone in the country. This, quite possibly, was how and when the idea for what became *The Lion, the Witch and the Wardrobe*, the first of the Narnia fantasies, took root. However, Lewis soon abandoned work on the original story and did not return to it for ten years.

Life at The Kilns took a new direction in 1950 when Mrs Moore, by now in her late seventies, was admitted to a nursing home. She died early the following year. Without the steadying influence of a woman about the place, Lewis lived the life of an unkempt, middle-aged bachelor don, sharing the house with Warnie and a cook. In many ways he had returned to the world of the undergraduate, though by now he was over fifty.

Lewis's chosen lifestyle left an indelible mark on The Kilns. The place reeked of tobacco and the walls were yellow with nicotine. The scruffy state of the house in many ways matched Lewis's own shabby appearance. He was not an immaculate or stylish dresser and he had an unfortunate habit of putting his lit pipe in his pocket so that it soon burned a hole in the material.

There had been few changes to the décor at The Kilns over the years; the curtains were worn and of the old blackout variety. Lewis could see no reason to change them. He was frugal but he was kind and generous, donating much of his income to individuals – widows and orphans in particular – rather than organizations.

The early 1950s – the decade of post-war austerity – made little impact at The Kilns. For much of this period Lewis concentrated on *The Chronicles of Narnia*, which began with *The Lion, The Witch and The Wardrobe* in 1950 and ended six years later with *The Last Battle*, for which he was awarded the Carnegie Medal. The stories produced a flood of fan mail. There had long been a steady stream of correspondence from his readers, but one day in January 1950 he received a letter from a woman that would change his life.

Joy Gresham was an American and a communist, born in New York of Jewish parents. Her marriage to William Gresham, by whom she had two sons, had long been unhappy as a result of his infidelity and alcohol addiction. Joy, who converted to Christianity in 1946, had worked for a time in Hollywood as a junior screen-writer for MGM. She had published a volume of poetry and written several novels. Two years after her initial letter to Lewis, the couple met. She was in England trying to find a publisher for her book *Smoke on the Mountain*.

With her marriage over, Joy moved to London. She and her two boys came to stay with Lewis at The Kilns and by now her presence was clearly beginning to have an effect on him. Lewis, seventeen years her senior, greatly enjoyed the time they were together but he found it exhausting. Joy struggled financially during this period and Lewis suggested that it would be economically beneficial for her to live in Oxford – in particular, at nearby Headington, a mile or so from The Kilns.

Meeting Joy Gresham awakened something in Lewis that perhaps had long been dead; he found her quick, responsive and stimulating and he was clearly attracted to her. She was in love with him. Joy moved from London to Headington in 1955 but their bliss-ful existence was doomed.

Following a fall, Joy was admitted to hospital where she was diagnosed with breast cancer. The prognosis was not good and she wasn't expected to live long. The devastating discovery made Lewis realize how much he loved Joy and wanted to marry her. The ceremony went ahead and the cancer that threatened to destroy their union so quickly thankfully entered a period of remission. For a time the death sentence was lifted.

Warnie and his newly married brother nursed Joy at The Kilns. She was bedridden much of the time but her razor-sharp wit provoked constant laughter, which echoed happily round the house. They found humour in the most humiliating and demeaning of circumstances. Even the bedpan yielded amusement. They named it Caliban from *The Tempest*.

Ultimately, Joy's cancer worsened and she died in hospital in 1960. She was forty-five. Their time together was short but wonderfully happy. Lewis died at The Kilns three years later, in November 1963, a week short of his sixty-fifth birthday. His health had been in steady decline for some months, his condition compounded by a heart attack in June. Lewis's death coincided, almost to the hour, with one of the most tragic and momentous events of the twentieth century – the assassination of President Kennedy in Dallas. Not unreasonably, Lewis's passing was afforded little press coverage.

Warnie died ten years later in 1973 and The Kilns was sold. The new owners made many changes within the house and the interior decorations reflected the period. The fireplaces and the chimneys were removed and the windows replaced. By 1984, however, the house was in a poor state of repair and up for sale once again.

Today The Kilns is owned by an American foundation and operates as a ecumenical community of graduate students and faculty, with a commitment to advance the intellectual and spiritual legacy of C.S. Lewis, one of the most influential popular writers and prominent Christian apologists of our age, through scholarship, reflection, writing and vibrant discussion. Within the confines of the house are conferences, day seminars and professional gatherings. The house has been restored to how it was during Lewis's tenure, its striking simplicity and unpretentious furnishings and décor recalling a very different world. Every week there is a steady flow of visitors to The Kilns and every week the callers include literary scholars and devotees of the Narnia stories whose respect for the author and his work remains undimmed.

C.S. Lewis 1898 –1963

The son of a solicitor, Clive Staples Lewis was born in Dundela, a suburb of Belfast. In 1916 he won a Classical scholarship to University College, Oxford. Lewis joined the Somerset Light Infantry and crossed to France in 1917. He was wounded at the Battle of Arras in 1918 and convalesced until the end of the war. He returned to Oxford in 1919 before taking up the position of Fellow and Tutor in English Language and Literature, a post he held for twenty-nine years. He taught Anglo-Saxon, philosophy and political theory and English literature. Lewis was initially agnostic but later committed himself to the Christian position.

Outwardly, Lewis fitted the image of the shambolic academic – a balding professorial figure with nicotine-stained teeth and fingers. However, the appearance belied the inner man. By nature Lewis was boisterous, humorous, ruddy and beery. He bore little resemblance to Anthony Hopkins's interpretation of him in the film *Shadowlands*, based on William Nicholson's play.

At Magdalen College, given his demeanour and somewhat tattered appearance, Lewis was often mistaken for a handyman or gardener. The distinguished actor Robert Hardy was an undergraduate at the college during the mid-1940s; Lewis was his tutor. On arrival at Magdalen, Hardy was terrified at the prospect of meeting the great man. One day, within the college precincts, the student spotted a figure approaching him, dressed in a scruffy jacket and corduroy bags. As the man passed, he turned and inquired: 'Are you Hardy?' It was C.S. Lewis, but Hardy was convinced at first that he was a college gardener. With Lewis's identity quickly established, the aspiring actor soon found his tutor to be humorous and joyful and the two men got on very well.

Lewis didn't drive – he failed his driving test seventeen times – so relied on his gardener and general factotum Fred Paxford, among others, to chauffeur him. Paxford, a genuine countryman who spoke with a distinctive Cotswold burr, became the model for Puddleglum in the Narnia story *The Silver Chair*. Paxford and Lewis were the same age.

In addition to the seven-title Narnia Chronicles, 85 million copies of which have been sold in twenty-nine languages, Lewis wrote *The Screwtape Letters* (1940), renowned for its religious theme and written in response to what Lewis saw as the threat of creeping atheism, and a science-fiction trilogy *Out of the Silent Planet* (1938), *Perelandra* (1939) and *That Hideous Strength* (1945). His first book of poems *Spirits in Bondage* was published in 1918.

A memorial to Lewis was formally unveiled in Poets' Corner in Westminster Abbey on 22 November 2013 to mark the fiftieth anniversary of his death. Dr Rowan Williams, the former Archbishop of Canterbury, gave the address.

MAPLEDURHAM HOUSE

THE RIVERBANK ADVENTURES OF Mole, Badger and Ratty and, of course, the exuberant Mr Toad, have a timeless appeal and the writer Kenneth Grahame's ability to endow the characters with endearing human traits and characteristics gives *The Wind in the Willows* a unique, magical quality.

Grahame used poetic licence and the brilliance and ingenuity of his own imagination to create those adventures, but an assortment of tantalizing clues and credible theories suggest he modelled the setting in the story on a stretch of the River Thames he knew from childhood and his later years.

Following the death of his mother when he was a small child, Grahame lived with his grandmother at Cookham Dean, near Maidenhead. In his final years he and his wife Elspeth settled upstream at Pangbourne, a picturesque village between Reading and Wallingford. Between the two villages, the Thames meanders through some of the loveliest landscape in the south of England.

Literary scholars have long pondered over the identity of the landmarks in Grahame's cherished masterpiece and therein lies the magic. Nothing can be proved conclusively and there are many devotees of the book who derive as much pleasure from reading it as they do from speculating over the precise whereabouts of the settings.

The Wild Wood is almost certainly Quarry Wood near Marlow, historic Reading Gaol might well have been the model for the prison where Toad was incarcerated, while the railway and the canal he journeyed along after escaping could easily be the mid-nineteenth century Brunel line running parallel to the Thames and the Kennet and Avon Canal at Reading.

Most contentious of all, however, is the whereabouts of Toad Hall. There are at least four houses on the Thames between Maidenhead and Pangbourne that might have inspired Kenneth Grahame, a favourite being Mapledurham House on the north bank of the river just outside Caversham.

Grahame's description of Toad Hall in the story strongly suggests the house and giving extra credence is the claim that when the author met E.S. Shepard, who produced the book's enchanting illustrations, he recommended the artist model Toad Hall on the mansion:

> Rounding a bend in the river they came in sight of a handsome, dignified old house of mellow red brick, with well-kept lawns reaching down to the water's edge. 'There's Toad Hall,' said the Rat ...' Toad is rather rich, you know, and this is really one of the nicest houses in these parts, though we never admit as much to Toad.'

Completed during the late sixteenth century by Sir Richard Blount for his Catholic family and built of red brick with stone dressings and an oak staircase, Mapledurham is one of the largest and most famous Elizabethan mansions in Oxfordshire. The house contains a priest hole and there is also a private chapel, visible from Mapledurham's adjacent fifteenth-century church of St Margaret.

Close to the outer suburbs of Reading, Mapledurham House occupies a delightful position on the Oxfordshire bank of the Thames. The name means 'maple tree enclosure'.

Between 1707 and 1715, Alexander Pope was a frequent visitor at Mapledurham. During that time he courted both Martha and her sister Theresa, daughters of the then owner, Lyster Blount. Pope, regarded as the greatest English poet of the eighteenth century, claimed to be in love with the sisters on alternate days until he fell out with Theresa. Martha was clearly his favourite and it was suggested they marry in secret. The two of them together must have presented an incongruous picture; he was only four feet six inches tall, while she was six feet.

Kenneth Grahame 1859–1932

The third of four children, Grahame was born in Edinburgh. He was five years of age when his mother died of scarlet fever. His father, an advocate, never recovered from the loss and spent most of his remaining years in France, leaving Kenneth to be raised by his maternal grandmother. He attended St Edward's School, Oxford, where he became head boy, and in 1879 he entered the Bank of England as a clerk; he later became one of its youngest secretaries.

Influenced by Robert Louis Stevenson, he wrote essays and then a short piece, *The Olympians*, a portrait of childhood, published in 1891. *The Golden Age* (1895) and *Dream Days* (1899) are acknowledged as subtle studies of the child's mind and imagination.

Grahame married Elspeth Thomson in 1899. In middle age, ill health forced him to retire from the Bank of England and he set about adapting a series of letters written to his only son, Alastair, into a fantasy novel that would appeal to children and adults and win the approval of President Theodore Roosevelt, among others. *The Wind in the Willows* was published in 1908 and has never been out of print.

Alexander Pope 1688–1744

The son of a Catholic wholesale linen merchant, Pope developed a tubercular infection of the spine at the age of twelve, which left him severely disabled and stunted his growth. Educated at various private schools, his first verses were published in 1709 and his *Essay on Criticism* (1711) brought him greater acclaim. Later work included *The Rape of the Lock* (1712) and *The Dunciad* (1728). In company with Gay, Swift and others, he formed the Scriblerus Club to write satire whose theme was the Whig establishment.

JANE AUSTEN'S HOUSE MUSEUM

FEW HOUSES DRAW AS many visitors as Chawton, the Hampshire home of Jane Austen, our most famous female novelist. Theories abound as to the layout of the house during Jane's time at Chawton, though much of it is essentially unaltered since her day. Dating back to the early sixteenth century and originally a farmhouse, today it is a museum, retaining the air and atmosphere of a modest country home of the early nineteenth century when the Austens resided here. Jane, her widowed mother and sister Cassandra lived at Chawton between 1809 and 1817. They were joined by their friend, Martha Lloyd, who had gone to live with the family in Southampton, following the death of her mother. Her sister, Mary, married James Austen, Jane's eldest brother.

Eight months before the Austens moved to Chawton, Jane wrote to Cassandra: 'There are six bed-chambers at Chawton. Henry [Jane's brother] wrote to my mother the other day and luckily mentioned the number, which is just what we want to be assured of. He speaks also of garrets with store-places.' So convinced was she of Chawton's suitability that she praised it in verse:

Our Chawton home, how much we find
Already in it to our mind;
And how convinced that when complete
It will all other houses beat
That ever have been made or mended
With rooms concise or rooms distended.

Edward Austen, the third eldest of Jane's brothers, who inherited the Godmersham Park estate in Kent and assumed the name Knight following the death of his adoptive mother in 1812, was the principal landowner in Chawton. Although he never lived in the village, he furnished the house and made the family reasonably comfortable. He also acquired a range, renewed the plumbing, and moved a window from the front of the building to the side to afford greater seclusion and a view of the garden. Edward permitted his mother and two sisters, very much the poor relations, to live rent-free in the house.

The Austens chose Chawton, which Jane described as 'a remark-ably pretty village', for several reasons. They knew the area, and the house was well placed for shopping in Alton, where Henry had opened a branch of his bank, and for visiting their old home at Steventon, twelve miles away, where James was rector. They lived contentedly at Chawton and, as the family of an affluent country squire, their social standing was assured.

Jane Austen's final years at Chawton were settled and happy. Built of redbrick and situated in the village centre, the house is known for its creaky doors and floors.

Jane Austen lived in the village for the last eight years of her short life and during that period she was especially productive. All the members of the household had their allotted duties. Cassandra and Martha undertook the main tasks, their mother concentrated on managing her beloved garden, a manservant was employed for the heavy work and there was a part-time cook. Jane prepared breakfast in the dining room every day at about nine o'clock. She was also an accomplished pianist and practised each morning before the family sat down to eat.

With Cassandra's help and support at Chawton, Jane was free to

The 12-sided walnut writing table where Jane Austen wrote can be seen by the window in the parlour. After her sister Cassandra's death in 1845, the table was given to a manservant.

write. She would sit at the little three-legged table, which she used as her writing desk, in the dining room and here, by the window she revised *Sense and Sensibility* and *Pride and Prejudice* prior to publication. At the front of the house, just a few feet from where she sat, was the main coaching route between London, Winchester, Gosport, Southampton and Portsmouth. While at Chawton Jane also began work on *Mansfield Park*, generally acknowledged as her masterpiece, and later wrote *Emma*. *Persuasion*, also written at Chawton, was published after her death. She started on *Sanditon* in January 1817 but did not live to complete it.

Jane Austen's desire to write influenced her daily routine, although the general business of the house was known to interrupt her concentration. There were the usual domestic duties and

119

household tasks to attend to, and there were also guests and visitors to look after. 'Composition seems to me Impossible with a head full of Joints of Mutton & doses of Rhubarb,' she wrote in a letter in September 1816.

Reading and walking also featured strongly in her life and she loved to explore the pretty countryside surrounding Chawton. She would occasionally walk to Alton, though mostly she and the family used the donkey carriage, which can be seen in the bakehouse.

Sometimes at the house she would be struck by a thought or an idea and would rush from the room to her writing desk. Visitors to Chawton soon become immersed in the long-vanished world of Jane Austen as they picture this literary genius out walking or writing at her desk, her mind wrestling with the finer points of plot detail and the complexities of her characters. The business of writing demanded much of her time and her head was never still.

As with most novelists, Jane Austen used poetic licence. Northanger Abbey, Mansfield Park and the other great houses of which she writes are the work of her imagination, but are clearly influenced by visits to country estates such as Godmersham and Goodnestone Park, near Canterbury, both of which symbolize the atmosphere of the time and Jane's mannered world of muslin frocks, imposing country houses and young suitors in tail coats.

Jane Austen's mother died in 1827 aged eighty-seven and is buried in the churchyard of St Nicholas's in Chawton. When Martha Lloyd married Jane's older brother Frank, who had been widowed, Cassandra continued to live at Chawton – now the sole occupant of the house. After her death in 1845 she, too, was buried in the village. The Austen's former home was then converted into three dwellings for estate workers. Later, several members of the Knight family lived at Chawton.

The house, now owned by the Jane Austen Memorial Trust, became a museum in the late 1940s. Between 1984 and 1994, thanks to the vision of Jean Bowden, a noted Austen scholar, a new era of change was ushered in at Chawton, transforming the house for the benefit of the museum's visitors and the novelist's loyal readers. A curator now oversees the day to day running of what is generally regarded as one of Britain's most important literary shrines.

Jane Austen 1775–1817

The seventh of eight children, Jane Austen was born at Steventon in Hampshire. Her scholarly father, who was rector of the parish, fulfilled the role of her tutor. Jane, who began to write in her teens, lived in the village for twenty-five years before the family moved to Bath. Although Jane found it difficult to adapt to living in the city, she turned the experience to good effect by using Bath as a setting for her novels.

After her father's death in 1805 Jane, her mother and her sister Cassandra returned to rural Hampshire. Her brother, Henry, helped her in her dealings with publishers and funded the publication of *Sense and Sensibility* in 1811. Published in 1813, *Pride and Prejudice*, was praised by Sir Walter Scott, and *Mansfield Park* (1814) is regarded as her greatest work, with its layered themes of privileged society and class struggle in Regency England.

Emma (1815) was dedicated to the Prince Regent, who admired her work. *Persuasion* and *Northanger Abbey* were published posthumously and twelve chapters are all that exist of her final unfinished work *Sanditon*.

A meticulous perfectionist in her writing, not unused to making substantial alterations to drafts of her stories and even changing the title, Jane Austen was also a shrewd and acute observer of human nature. She is credited with pioneering the modern novel and influencing many generations of novelists. Thanks largely to modern-day film and television adaptations of her work, her name lives on.

GILBERT WHITE'S HOUSE

BELOW THE MIGHTY BEECH trees of Selborne Hanger, in the main street of the picturesque village of Selborne, stands The Wakes, the home of the eighteenth-century naturalist Gilbert White, the highly respected and much revered father of ecology. Situated on the northern edge of the South Downs, not far from Hampshire's border with Sussex, the village's gloriously wooded setting remains as charming and unspoiled as it would have been in his day – 'the Mecca of naturalists and nature lovers, the living green outdoor laboratory of Gilbert White. Over every inch his quick and eager ghost presides.' This eloquent description appears in a 1973 National Trust guide to Britain but still resonates today.

The Wakes lies in the shadow of Selborne Hanger, where delightful paths meander between mighty beeches.

White, who regularly recorded anything of significance in his notebook while out working in the garden or walking locally, hated the harsh winters of the late eighteenth century, although he was a dedicated horticulturalist. He cultivated his own produce, became the first gardener in the area to grow potatoes, and made beer and wine in the brew house. As curate of Selborne, White was actively involved in the life of the community, and although he never married, he loved to surround himself with family and friends. He also enjoyed the companionship of animals and among his pets were Timothy, a tortoise, a pony called Mouse and several dogs, including a spaniel known as Fairey Queen.

Little escaped White's attention and he was known to record significant events in the story of Selborne. In 1756 he wrote in his journal: 'Planted four limes in the butcher's yard to hide the sight of blood and filth from the windows.' Two of the original four trees still survive, as does the butcher's slaughterhouse behind, which remained in use until the First World War.

One of White's undeniable pleasures was strolling the leafy glades and secluded paths near his home in search of the local flora and fauna. The nearby Selborne Hanger was described by White as 'a vast hill of chalk rising 300 feet above the village, and is ... divided into a sheep down, the high wood, and a long hanging wood called the Hanger. The cover of this eminence is altogether beech, the most lovely of all forest trees.' The Zigzag Path, which climbs to the top of the hanger, was cut by White and his brother in 1753 as a short cut to the summit.

Much of The Wakes dates back to the seventeenth century; it was originally a traditional, timber-framed building. The house was bought by White's grandfather, whose name was also Gilbert, at the beginning of the eighteenth century. The Wakes was extended in 1725 and when White inherited the house nearly forty years later, he added the brew house and the great parlour.

It was in the 1950s, more than a century and a half after White's passing, that The Wakes was put up for sale. Enthusiasts desperately tried to raise sufficient funds to safeguard its future. Eventually, in 1955, help came from an unexpected quarter. Robert Oates, cousin of the polar explorer Lawrence, provided the financial wherewithal to buy the house and thus save it for the nation. Today, the house is

The Wakes was the cherished home of Gilbert White, a pioneer in the field of English natural history. The house includes furnished rooms and delicately embroidered bed hangings.

a museum devoted to the memory of Gilbert White, Captain Oates and his uncle Francis Oates, a Victorian naturalist and explorer. White and the two Oates were not related, although they shared common characteristics as pioneers and devotees of the great outdoors.

Inside the house is Gilbert White's study, which has been furnished and designed to reflect his wide-ranging interests. The large drop-leaf table belonged to him and the academic gown recalls his student days at Oxford. White was a compulsive letter writer and corresponded regularly with friends and relatives. It was in this room, too, that he wrote his sermons.

Gilbert White 1720–93

An extremely gifted man, Gilbert White was a curate and an Oxford don. His father was a barrister and his grandfather vicar of the parish of Selborne. Born in the village, White studied at Oxford, later becoming a fellow and Dean of Oriel. During his time at university he spent much of his time playing cards, riding, boating, shooting and attending concerts. He was ordained in 1746 and later appointed the perpetual curate of Moreton Pinkney in Northamptonshire. In 1743 he returned to Selborne, the place of his birth, where he became curate for the remainder of his life. Gilbert White is buried in Selborne churchyard, a short distance from his beloved home in the village.

White's masterpiece is *The Natural History of Selborne*, a lovingly crafted, meticulously detailed study of the natural world on his own doorstep in the form of letters written to leading naturalists of the day. First published in 1788, five years before White's death, it has been the subject of countless editions and translated into French, Danish, Swedish and Japanese. The original, beautifully composed manuscript was sold at Christie's in 1980 for £100,000.

White represents the link between ourselves and the extraordinary world of natural history, of creation itself. Through his acquired knowledge and experience, we can learn from him about the cycle of the seasons, the process of evolution and the natural landscape around us teeming with myriad life forms. Few naturalists have made such an impact on the civilized world; over two hundred years after his death, he is still remembered, still celebrated. Greatly inspired by White and having read *The Natural History of Selborne*, Charles Darwin pondered: 'why every gentleman did not become an ornithologist'. David Attenborough describes him as 'a man in total harmony with his world'.

HUGHENDEN MANOR

WHEN BENJAMIN DISRAELI ACQUIRED Hughenden Manor in 1848, it was a very different house – a brick-built, white-painted, three-storeyed Georgian building of simple design and unpretentious appearance. The house, set on the slope of a hill and overlooking woods and parkland, was Gothicized by the architect E.B. Lamb in 1862, with the west wing added by Disraeli's nephew, Coningsby, in 1910.

However, intended improvements did little to transform the style of Hughenden. Nikolaus Pevsner, the art historian and well-respected authority on English architecture, was one of the fiercest critics, describing the redbrick re-facing of the outside as 'excruciating, everything sharp, angular and aggressive – window-heads indescribable'.

Alhough architectural historians have long regarded Hughenden as a plain, undistinguished house, Disraeli felt it perfectly fulfilled his needs and requirements. He chose Hughenden as his country home for several reasons. He won the seat of Bucks in 1847 and it was important for a rising politician to live within the constituency, especially as the move coincided with a major boost in Disraeli's political fortunes. He became leader of the Conservatives in the House of Commons, then Leader of the House and Chancellor of the Exchequer before finally securing the role of Prime Minister in 1868. Queen Victoria conferred the title of 1st Earl of Beaconsfield on Disraeli in 1876.

Hughenden, conveniently close to his father's rented home at Bradenham, lay at the heart of his 'beloved and beechy Bucks'. Disraeli had known the Chilterns since boyhood: 'I am not surprised that the ancients worshipped Trees', he wrote. He assumed the role of the country squire and would spend much of his time at Hughenden walking in the woods and surveying his 750-acre estate.

However, the image of the affluent landowner was somewhat misleading. Disraeli was by no means a wealthy man, although nine years before he bought Hughenden, he had married Mary Anne, the rich widow of Wyndham Lewis, an old colleague from his early years in politics. Disraeli's wife was twelve years his senior but it was a successful union. The house was bought with the help of a loan of £35,000.

By the time he moved to Hughenden, Disraeli was also an established novelist who commanded sizeable advances and much publicity thanks to his significant role in British politics. His best-known work, though the canon is largely forgotten today, is almost certainly the trilogy *Coningsby*, *Sybil* and *Tancred* all written in the 1840s, the same decade that saw Disraeli move to Hughenden, and signalled he was destined for higher office. These autobiographical novels reflect Disraeli's writing at its best – a striking mix of social and political themes influenced by personal observations he made during a tour of the North of England in 1844. Disraeli believed it was as a novelist that he could most effectively sway public opinion.

Disraeli may have used his writing as a way of influencing the mood or perspective of the electorate but it almost certainly did little to impress his nemesis, the Liberal leader William Gladstone, who disliked Disraeli's imperialism and grand notions of Empire. It was Disraeli who turned Queen Victoria against Gladstone, whilst establishing his own close and touching association with the monarch at a time when, crucially, she needed the support and trust of others. (Following the death of Prince Albert in 1861, Victoria withdrew from public life to mourn his passing.)

As the years passed, Victoria became an increasingly distant and reclusive figure – isolated from her family and her subjects. It was Disraeli who encouraged her back into public life, helping to restore her confidence and giving her the strength to continue. The study at Hughenden Manor, filled with letters and manuscripts, illustrates the friendship and respect that existed between them. Victoria spent some time in Disraeli's study after his funeral and afterwards wrote movingly about her visits to the house in her journal, dated 30 April, 1881:

We got into the carriage and drove up to the house. All was just the same as when, two and a half years ago, dear Lord Beaconsfield received us there. Such a sad contrast. We went into the library and the drawing room, where hangs my picture, all the same only he is not there! Took tea in the library where I had sat with my kind friend and where he had given me an account of a very stormy cabinet he had had. I seem to hear his voice and the impassioned, eager way he described everything.

Elsewhere in the house there are reminders of Disraeli's literary aspirations and his love of books. 'I have a passion for books and trees,' he wrote. 'I like to look at them. When I come down to Hughenden, I pass the first week in sauntering about my park and examining all the trees and then I saunter in the library and survey the books.' He inherited his father's vast library of 25,000 volumes.

The Garden Hall at Hughenden includes a portrait of Lord Byron whom Disraeli idolized, and the Statesman's Room has copies of photographs and documents illustrating his political triumphs. Disraeli's desk is covered with papers and maps of the world. A tour of Hughenden, now in the care of the National Trust, also includes the library where he relaxed and conducted his business affairs.

Three rooms on the top floor, housing a number of rarely seen items belonging to Disraeli, were opened to visitors in 2013. Among them are the original handwritten manuscript of his novel *Sybil* and the robes and ceremonial shoes of his earldom. The rooms, previously used as staff offices, offer impressive views of Hughenden's formal gardens.

Benjamin Disraeli 1804–81

Born in London, the baptized elder son of a Spanish Jew, Disraeli was educated at a private school in Walthamstow by a Unitarian minister. He was later articled to a solicitor and attended nine terms at Lincoln's Inn. By the age of twenty, Disraeli had abandoned law in favour in politics. Clever and ambitious, he was also a superb orator and a gifted writer and wit. 'When I want to read a novel I write one,' he said when, following the publication of George Eliot's *Daniel Deronda* in 1876, someone asked if he had read it. Fiercely political, his main objectives in life were to further the cause of the workers, popularize the monarchy and foster the might, unity and glory of the British Empire.

He entered parliament in 1837, representing the constituency of Maidstone in Kent. However, his flamboyant style of dress and reputation as a dandy brought howls of derision in the House when he stood to make his maiden speech.

Disraeli's career as a novelist began long before he became a politician. His first book *Vivian Grey* (1826) satirizes leading figures of the day, including the noted publisher, John Murray.

Disraeli abandoned his writing career while he ascended the political ladder but returned to it following his resignation as Prime Minister. Newspaper journalists were agog, keen to see how successfully the former statesman would revive his fortunes as a novelist. His new book was *Lothair* (1870), in which Disraeli took as his subject the power of the Catholic Church in England. 'Mr Disraeli has provided a new sensation for a jaded public,' proclaimed one article. 'The English mind was startled when a retired novelist became Prime Minister. It has been not less surprised … that a retired Prime Minister is about again to become a novelist.'

Events were repeated ten years later when Disraeli resigned as Prime Minister for the second time and once again re-launched his career as a novelist. But by now he was approaching the end of his life and there was only one more novel in him, which, like *Lothair*, was written at Hughenden. *Endymion* was published in 1880, a year before his death, yielding him an advance of £10,000 – an incredible sum for a book in those days. The story was influenced by Disraeli's early years in politics and satirized many leading figures of the day. Even Dickens is caricatured, featuring as 'Gushy', an overtly sentimental novelist.

Disraeli often modelled the houses in his novels on real places. Chatsworth and Welbeck Abbey apparently inspired Coningsby Castle, and Beaumanoir, featured in *Sybil*, is Belvoir Castle.

Disraeli is remembered as a politician who transformed the Conservative Party. Not surprisingly, his achievements in government largely eclipsed his second career as a writer. Examining Disraeli's work today, however, offers the reader a fascinating glimpse of the machinations of Victorian politics, the privileged lives of those who sought to manipulate the system and the plight of the working classes.

OLD THATCH

OLD THATCH IS A quintessentially English seventeenth-century cottage in the heart of the Home Counties; the sort of place that represents a chocolate-box England of village greens and winding country lanes. Given her spirit of Englishness and the moral tone and cosy, middle-class world of her books, it seems apt, therefore, that one of Britain's best-known and most celebrated children's authors, Enid Blyton, should have lived in this charming thatched cottage in the years leading up to the Second World War. Even today, more than seventy-five years after she left Old Thatch, her spirit is evident.

Enid Blyton stumbled on Old Thatch, a Grade II listed building, in the summer of 1929 when, just before her thirty-second birthday, she and her husband Hugh Pollock began searching for a new home in the area. The cottage captivated Blyton from the moment she saw it and in her diary she described it as a very old house rather like a rambling cottage. 'It is perfect both outside and in,' she wrote. 'Just like a Fairy Tale House.'

Enid Blyton loved Old Thatch, the inspiration for *The Mystery of the Burnt Cottage*, published in 1943.

Blyton went ahead and bought Old Thatch. A month after moving in, she was offered a regular full page in *Teacher's World*, a weekly publication for the teaching profession of which she was once a member. 'Enid Blyton's Children's Page', as it was known, always featured an illustration of Old Thatch and a photograph usually supplied by Blyton – often of the cottage garden or one of her pets.

Blyton's column, which always began with 'Dear girls and boys', represented an effective form of communication with her many readers. She covered all manner of subjects – from poetry to the changing seasons – and she regularly received letters from both children and teachers. One child wrote to her saying: 'If you go on writing nice poems you will be quite famous one day'. Blyton's biographer, Barbara Stoney, wrote that '… it was not surprising that the small village post office in Well End soon found that the mail to Old Thatch warranted a special delivery.'

'Enid Blyton's Children's Page' also included a letter from Bobs, her much-loved fox-terrier, describing family life through the eyes of a cherished pet. The letters from Bobs proved to be so popular that Blyton continued to include them in the column long after the dog's death. The letters were published in book form in 1933, with 10,000 copies sold in the first week.

Blyton described Old Thatch and its garden in great detail in *Teacher's World* so that her readers were left with a vivid picture of the enchanting cottage and its setting. In one edition she wrote:

> Now I promised to tell you about the garden of the dear little cottage I found, didn't I? Well, it really is simply lovely. It is about nine times as big as the garden of Elfin Cottage [her old home] and you could almost get lost in it. You enter through a funny old lych-gate and you find yourself sideways to the cottage. Roses bloom everywhere – there are dozens, all hanging gracefully down, a mass of brilliant colour.

Blyton also writes about Old Thatch in her autobiography *The Story of my Life* (1952), explaining that the cottage took its name from the thatched roof in which innumerable wrens nested:

One of the bedrooms I made into a nursery and what a nursery it was – none other than the bedroom in which Dick Turpin slept when he rode in his usual haunts round about Maidenhead Thicket. When Old Thatch was an inn, there was one bedroom kept for travellers and many a time, so I was told, Black Bess was put into the stables downstairs (my bedroom) while Dick Turpin slept peacefully in the room where my children now played each day.

Blyton, who wrote very quickly – often managing up to 6,000 words per day on her trusty typewriter – frequently expressed her fondness for Old Thatch. 'It was a lovely place to write stories ... but it was soon too small for a growing family,' she wrote. 'Look at it and you'll be sure to recognize it in my books.' By the mid-1930s, Blyton was the mother of two daughters, Gillian and Imogen, but her output continued unabated.

One book above all other Enid Blyton titles was clearly inspired by her former home in the Thames Valley. *The Mystery of the Burnt Cottage* (1943) features a traditional country cottage at the heart of the story and introduces a group of children known as the Five

Old Thatch has a glorious, expertly managed garden.

Find-Outers. These characters never caught the public imagination in quite the same way as, say, the Famous Five, nevertheless they were popular with devoted readers. Although Blyton had left Old Thatch by the time the first title in the series was published, it is obvious from the description of the cottage that she modelled it on her former home.

Enid Blyton led an active social life while living in Buckinghamshire. She regularly hosted dinner parties and bridge matches at the cottage, while tennis featured among her more energetic leisure pursuits. However, after nearly ten years at Old Thatch, fault lines were beginning to undermine her idyllic life here. As war loomed, so her marriage began to disintegrate and she and Hugh later divorced. Blyton moved to Green Hedges, a much larger family home near Beaconsfield, remarrying in 1943.

Old Thatch's present owners, renowned garden designer Jacky Hawthorne and her husband David, bought the cottage in 1994 and have since devoted a great deal of time and energy to transforming the garden, which remained largely derelict until 2000. Their intention was to capture the spirit of the place while retaining elements of the old garden. A great deal of modern and traditional planting has taken place over the years and among a host of striking and colourful features are a water garden, a lavender terrace and a rose and clematis walk.

However, despite the radical changes, there are still tangible reminders of Blyton's time there. For example, the yew hedge and the old well, seen in photographs of Blyton at Old Thatch, are instantly familiar to fans who often arrive unannounced, or tour the gardens during the prescribed times. Others who visit are initially unaware of the literary connection but are soon wallowing in childhood memories as they recall the magical, rose-tinted world of Enid Blyton.

Enid Blyton 1897–1968

Born in London, Enid Blyton trained as a kindergarten teacher before working as a journalist specializing in educational and children's publications. Her first book *Child Whispers*, a collection of verse, was published in 1922 but her career began in earnest in the late 1930s when she started to produce the much-loved children's stories for which she is best remembered – among them the *Malory Towers* series. The dust jackets of some editions of her books would describe her as Britain's best-loved and most popular children's author, citing her two daughters as her earliest critics and most ardent fans.

Blyton was a prolific writer who created a fantasy world of innocence and adventure for generations of children. Her books are still widely read today and she has been the subject of several biographies and documentaries. Through her work, Blyton has left her loyal audience a wonderful legacy; those of us of a certain age who read her books avidly as youngsters now look upon her stories with a very real sense of nostalgia. Blyton's output is staggering. She published more than six hundred books with Noddy, the Famous Five and the Secret Seven among her most cherished and enduring characters. In more recent years, however, her reputation has been sullied somewhat by accusations of racism, sexism, snobbery, xenophobia, limited vocabulary and a lack of style. Afflicted by dementia in later life, she died in a nursing home in Hampstead, aged seventy-one.

MILTON'S COTTAGE

A MODEST TIMBER-FRAMED COTTAGE beside a main road in the Chilterns is the somewhat unexpected setting for John Milton's rural retreat and workplace. It was here, in these simple surroundings, that he completed *Paradise Lost* and began *Paradise Regained*.

Grade I-listed Milton's Cottage – the only surviving building in which the great English poet and parliamentarian lived – dates back to the sixteenth century and contains four main ground floor museum rooms which, with the help of many historic artefacts and against the contrasting sounds of birdsong and passing traffic, tell in fascinating detail the story of John Milton's life and explain the circumstances that brought him here.

Milton stayed at Chalfont St Giles while the Great Plague swept through London. The cottage belonged to the daughter of the regicide, George Fleetwood.

In 1665, with the Great Plague devastating London, Milton decided the best way to escape the disease was to leave the capital and seek sanctuary in the country. His Quaker friend and former Latin pupil Thomas Ellwood found him a 'pretty box' at 'Giles Chalfont'. Milton moved here from his home near Bunhill Fields in the City, accompanied by his third wife, Elizabeth Minshull. The picturesque cottage, which was rented by Ellwood on Milton's behalf and surrounded by rolling Chiltern hills, was in sharp contrast to his London home. However, a tragic irony overshadowed his new life in the country – Milton had been totally blind since about 1652 and never saw the cottage.

The poet lived at Chalfont St Giles for less than two years and during his time at the cottage he returned to *Paradise Lost*, which he had abandoned in 1642 in order to focus his energies on the Parliamentary cause in the English Civil War. Over twenty years later, and far away from the chaos and confusion of a London stricken by plague, he was able to return to his unfinished work, although the isolation of the cottage plunged him into a solitary, silent world far removed from his life in the capital. Milton's blindness, too, gave his imagination and writing a very different perspective.

Thomas Ellwood wrote about Milton's move to the country and the completion of *Paradise Lost* in his autobiography *The History of the Life of Thomas Ellwood*:

> I soon made a visit to him [Milton] to welcome him into the country. After some common discourse had passed between us, he called for a manuscript of his; which being brought he delivered to me, bidding me to take it home with me, and read it at my leisure; and when I had done so return it to him with my judgment thereupon. When I came home and had set myself to read it, I found it was that excellent poem which he entitled 'Paradise Lost'.
>
> After I had, with the best attention, read it through, I made him another visit, and returned him his book, with due acknowledgement of the favour he had done me in communicating it to me. He asked me how I liked it and what I thought of it, which I modestly but freely told him, and after some further discourse about it, I pleasantly said to him, 'Thou hast said much here of "Paradise Lost", but what hast thou to say of "Paradise Found"?' He made me no answer, but sat some time in a muse; then broke off that discourse, and fell upon another subject.

When London was finally purged of disease, Milton returned to the capital, only to receive a visit from Ellwood. Milton showed his visitor *Paradise Regained*, telling him, 'This is owing to you for you put it into my head by the question you put to me at Chalfont, which before I had not thought of.'

Some aspects of the original cottage remain, helping the visitor to imagine what it was like when Milton lived here. A tour of it today – 350 years after his tenancy – reveals much about the poet and his life during his brief period at Chalfont St Giles. Milton's study, where he slept and finished *Paradise Lost*, can be seen; among the relics are a portrait of Milton attributed to the artist Godfrey Kneller and painted from memory, a Jacobean table, a Cromwellian chair, a lock of the poet's hair and a painted oak and cane chair thought to have belonged to him. There are also first editions of most of Milton's works.

The well-stocked garden, which, sadly, Milton could only visualize in his imagination, remains a charming feature of the cottage. Although he couldn't see them, the scent and the touch of the many herbs and flowers inspired Milton's writing. The garden contains a 400-year-old well and it is said that on a hot summer's day in 1666 Thomas Ellwood was seen to draw a beaker of water from it and present it to Gulielma Springett, his sweetheart, who later married William Penn, founder of Pennsylvania and a noted Quaker.

John Milton has influenced and inspired countless writers over the years – among them Jane Austen, Charles Dickens and the Brontë sisters. It seems fitting, therefore, that a decision was made in the 1880s to purchase the cottage and dedicate it to the memory of Milton, its former tenant. An appeal was launched – Queen Victoria donated £20 – the funds were raised and once the sale had been completed, the cottage was placed into the care of a committee of management. Acknowledged as one of the world's most important

Blindness denied Milton the chance to see his rural retreat in Buckinghamshire. The cottage garden at Chalfont St Giles is still a blaze of colour, 350 years after he stayed here.

literary shrines, with fifty per cent of its visitors from overseas, Milton's Cottage is now managed by a full-time curator responsible to eleven trustees.

John Milton 1608–74

Born in Bread Street in Cheapside, Milton was the son of a London scrivener – a notary and moneylender. He was educated at St Paul's School and Cambridge University. He planned to enter the Church but his increasing dismay over the state of the Anglican clergy influenced his decision to abandon the idea. Instead, he studied the Classics and ecclesiastical and political history in anticipation of a career as a poet. In the late 1630s he toured France and Italy and, on his return to London, he wrote a series of social, religious and political tracts. In 1642 he married Mary Powell, who died ten years later in childbirth.

During the English Civil War Milton supported Parliament and produced propaganda defending Charles I's execution. He married his second wife Katherine Woodcock in 1656; she died two years later. Milton's third wife was Elizabeth Minshull, whom he married in 1663. *Paradise Lost* was published in 1667 and *Paradise Regained* in 1671. He died, probably of renal failure associated with gout, and is buried beside his father near the altar in St Giles, Cripplegate.

THE MIDLANDS

MADRESFIELD COURT

IT IS OFTEN SAID that *Brideshead Revisited*, described as the most nostalgic and reflective of Evelyn Waugh's novels, recalling the gilded, halcyon days of the nobility in the inter-war years, evokes images of the baroque grandeur of Castle Howard. The magnificent house in North Yorkshire was the location for the film and television adaptations of the book, but that is where its link with *Brideshead Revisited* ends. Castle Howard matched Waugh's description of Brideshead Castle in the novel but it was the spirit of a very different house that sparked his imagination.

Evelyn Waugh modelled the Marchmain ancestral seat on Madresfield Court at the foot of the Malvern Hills, home of the Lygon family (pronounced Liggon) and the Earls of Beauchamp since the Middle Ages. In *Brideshead Revisited* (1945), the story's middle-class narrator, Charles Ryder, befriends whimsical Sebastian Flyte, son of the elegiac Lord Marchmain, at Oxford. Ryder's infatuation with the deeply flawed, Catholic Marchmain family and the enchanted, grandiose house they inhabit lies at the core of the novel. Waugh met the ethereally beautiful Hugh Lygon, the model for Sebastian, when they were undergraduates at Oxford in the early 1920s, and first set eyes on Madresfield Court in 1931 when he was invited to stay at the house.

Brideshead Revisited is defined by its strong religious themes – the pointlessness of human existence without God. However, the book can also be seen as a lament for the last days of Empire, for the dying vestiges of the old order and the decline of Britain's great estates.

Waugh broke his leg in parachute training in 1943 and was granted three months' leave without pay to write the novel, which he

The view from the moat, which allows visitors access to Madresfield Court. Inside the house are various portraits and photographs of the Lygon family.

completed the following summer. In the 1960 edition of *Brideshead Revisited* Waugh writes:

> It was impossible to foresee, in the spring of 1944, the present cult of the English country house. It seemed then that the ancestral seats, which were our chief national artistic achievement, were doomed to decay and spoliation like the monasteries in the sixteenth century. So I piled it on rather, with passionate sincerity. Brideshead today would be open to trippers, its treasures rearranged by expert hands and the fabric better maintained than it was by Lord Marchmain.

Waugh also wrote that his theme was 'the operation of divine grace on a group of diverse but closely connected characters'. He accepted, too, that the book was 'infused with a kind of gluttony, for food and wine, for the splendours of the recent past, and for rhetorical and ornamental language, which now with a full stomach I find distasteful'.

Madresfield Court welcomes visitors strictly by appointment. They begin their tour of the house by crossing the splendid mediaeval moat, which contains the renowned Malvern spring water. Had Britain been invaded by enemy forces in 1940, as feared, the house and its surroundings would have become familiar to a future monarch and her sister. Contingency plans were drawn up in 1938 to evacuate the two princesses, Elizabeth and Margaret, together with other members of the Royal Household, to Madresfield Court. In due course they would have departed for Canada, flying from one of the nearby airfields.

Nearly ten years before the storm clouds of war gathered over Madresfield, a brilliant young novelist, who was undergoing a period of significant change in his life, would have crossed the same moat. Evelyn Waugh had recently divorced his wife and converted to Catholicism when he first came to stay there. Twenty-eight years of age, Waugh had no fixed abode or, as he put it, 'no possessions which could not conveniently go on a porter's barrow'. Through his friendship with the drunken, dysfunctional Hugh, which some have suggested was a physical relationship, the house became an integral part of Waugh's life. He adopted the Lygon family in all but name and was in awe of its glamour and mystique from the moment he set foot on Madresfield turf.

Waugh set Brideshead Castle in Wiltshire but his description of Charles Ryder's first visit there, seeing the house rising out of the landscape and attempting to comprehend the sheer scale of the place and what it represented, was inspired by the moment Waugh himself was captivated by the magic and splendour of Madresfield Court:

We drove on and in the early afternoon came to our destination: wrought-iron gates and twin, Classical lodges on a village green, an avenue, more gates, open park-land, a turn in the drive; and suddenly a new and secret landscape opened before us. We were at the head of a valley and below us, half a mile distant, grey and gold amid a screen of boskage, shone the dome and columns of an old house.

'Well?' said Sebastian, stopping the car. Beyond the dome lay receding steps of water and round it, guarding and hiding it, stood the soft hills.

'Well?'

'What a place to live in!' I said.

Over subsequent years Waugh often travelled to Madresfield by train, met at Worcester by Maimie, one of the three Lygon daughters. Physically, Maimie was not unlike her brother, Hugh. Blonde and beautiful with perfectly proportioned even features, she was the height of glamour and sophistication. Waugh modelled the character of Julia Flyte, Sebastian's sister, on Maimie, but though he adored her he lacked the confidence to pursue her romantically.

Dating back to the twelfth century and characterized by neo-Gothic gables and mullioned windows, Madresfield Court was remodelled in the Victorian era to resemble a Tudor moated manor. A tour of the red-brick house reveals an impressive collection of porcelain,

Unlike the fictional Brideshead Castle, Madresfield Court is no aristocratic palace; yet for Evelyn Waugh, when he wrote *Brideshead Revisited* in 1944, the house represented a blissful memory of a time that he knew had passed.

furniture, paintings and family memorabilia. The house has 136 rooms and the estate amounts to 4,000 acres, including 500 acres of woodland.

One of the key features at Madresfield is the chapel, built as part of the 1865 re-creation of the house. The highlight is the striking Edwardian Arts and Craft decoration commissioned in 1902 by the wife of the 7th Earl as a present to her husband. Murals and frescoes adorn the walls, featuring the Lygon children depicted as flawless, cherubic figures amid flowers found in the gardens of Madresfield. Waugh's chapel in *Brideshead Revisited* is almost identical save for a couple of minor details:

> The whole interior had been gutted, elaborately refurnished and redecorated in the Arts-and-Crafts style of the last decade of the nineteenth century. Angels in printed cotton smocks, rambler-roses, flower-spangled meadows, frisking lambs, texts in Celtic script, saints in armour, covered the walls in an intricate pattern of clear, bright colours.
>
> 'Golly', I said.
>
> 'It was Papa's wedding present to Mamma. Now, if you've seen enough, we'll go.'

The Long Gallery, a relic of the old house, now includes the writing desk where Evelyn Waugh wrote *Black Mischief*, his comic novel about a mythical African king educated at an English university. Writing in the old day nursery at Madresfield, he completed the book in May 1932, shutting himself away for a few hours each day for enforced periods of creativity and solitude. However, the Lygon sisters, not inclined to appreciate the onerous task of writing a book, frequently interrupted his flow.

Although Waugh was clearly inspired by Madresfield when he wrote *Brideshead Revisited*, the comparison with Hetton Abbey in *A Handful of Dust* (1934) is more obvious. In the book, in which Waugh satirizes the landed gentry, Hetton is portrayed as a rambling Victorian mansion remodelled in the Gothic style. Like Madresfield Court, it boasted a moat and a central clock tower.

Evelyn Waugh was fortunate to stumble on the Lygons and

witness life at Madresfield Court. For a writer, the house and its family offered a glittering treasure-trove of ideas and material. In essence, Evelyn Waugh *was* Charles Ryder: the outsider looking in; the observer; a middle-class man who finds Arcadia peopled by beautiful, doomed souls. Waugh's stroke of genius was creating Ryder to act as the prism that reveals this extraordinary hedonistic world to the reader.

Evelyn Waugh 1903–66

The son of a publisher and editor, Evelyn Waugh was educated at Lancing and Oxford. After graduating he worked as a schoolmaster, where he gained material and inspiration for his first and highly successful novel *Decline and Fall* (1928). After a brief and unsuccessful marriage, he became a Roman Catholic in 1930. The themes of social satire and high comedy run through his later books, focusing on the cynical, carefree attitudes of the post-war generation. Waugh married a second time in 1937 and the following year published *Scoop*, one of his best-known novels. During World War Two he was posted to Crete and Yugoslavia, and his experiences there inspired the Sword of Honour trilogy – *Men at Arms* (1952), *Officers and Gentlemen* (1955) and *Unconditional Surrender* (1961). Waugh also wrote two travel books – *Labels* (1930) and *Remote People* (1931).

Urbane and witty and, by today's standards, a fearful snob, Evelyn Waugh was very much a product of his time. The younger brother of Alec Waugh, a noted novelist and travel writer, he died of a coronary thrombosis.

SHAKESPEARE'S BIRTHPLACE

ON THE SURFACE THE American showman Phineas T. Barnum seems an unlikely name to be associated with the very English culture of William Shakespeare. Implausible as it sounds, Barnum threatened to remove one of the key landmarks in the story of the great playwright and profit it by it in his native country.

In 1847, the half-timbered house where Shakespeare was born was put up for sale and, reputedly, when the extravagant Barnum heard the news, he decided he would buy the building, carefully dismantle it and ship it to the United States, where he would rebrand his precious cargo as one of North America's leading visitor attractions. He knew it would be a mammoth undertaking, but the potential was huge. Shakespeare was big business in any land.

Charles Dickens, one of the Bard's more celebrated devotees, led a campaign to raise £3,000 to buy the house and safeguard its future, thus preventing Barnum from realizing his somewhat vulgar ambition. Many eminent literary figures endorsed Dickens's crusade and there was even support from Prince Albert. Shakespeare's reputation as a literary genius could not be overestimated. The necessary funds were raised and the house, in a rather dilapidated state of repair at the time, was saved. That same year, the Shakespeare Birthplace Trust was established, with further fund-raising leading to the appointment of a custodian.

Dickens and his contemporaries were thus instrumental in securing the future of Shakespeare's birthplace. Without their efforts, visitors in subsequent years might well have been denied the chance

The house in Henley Street where William Shakespeare was born. Charles Dickens and many other distinguished writers were influential in saving Shakespeare's birthplace for the nation, preventing the house from being sold and shipped to the United States.

to see his childhood home. This is the house where it is assumed that Shakespeare, the eldest son and third of eight children, enjoyed his formative years.

It was in 1552 that his parents John and Mary Shakespeare moved to the house that was to become William's birthplace. His father was a wool merchant and glove-maker and he ran the business from the family home in Henley Street. At the time the Shakespeare family lived here, the house was part of a terrace. However, when the Birthplace Trust acquired it, a decision was taken to remove the adjoining buildings to reduce the risk of fire. The site included a bustling workshop where tanning took place and many of the young apprentices lived in the rafters. What is now a pleasant garden for visitors to explore at the rear of the house was originally a midden.

Dating back to the early 1530s, the building reflects William's childhood years, but more specifically it depicts the house when he was aged around ten. The parlour was where the family members gathered in the evening, settling themselves around the blazing fire. Traditionally, as this was the warmest room in the house, it also served as a guest bedroom. The hall where everyone would have eaten was small and cramped. The adults and senior members of the household sat, while the children stood. From the house William would have set off every day to school. Though once affluent and a respected member of the Stratford community, by now William's father was in serious financial difficulties. By a stroke of good fortune, his civic position as bailiff and a member of the town council entitled his son to be educated free of charge.

The year 1579 – when William was fifteen – was a significant date in his early life. With his grammar school education complete, he experienced the tragic loss of his younger sister Anne, who died of plague at the age of eight. Her death was a bitter blow at such a young age.

William Shakespeare was eighteen when he married Anne Hathaway and the couple initially lived at the family home in Henley Street. The house remained in the possession of the Shakespeare family for two subsequent centuries, during which time it was an alehouse. In 1806 it was sold to Thomas Court, a butcher.

A bust of Shakespeare, a copy of the larger memorial bust at Stratford-upon-Avon's Holy Trinity Church, has been on display at the writer's birthplace since around 1870. Its provenance is unknown.

Long before the Birthplace Trust rescued the house in Henley Street for the nation and the modern concept of tourism was created, Stratford was drawing large crowds; among them literary scholars who wanted to absorb the atmosphere of the place and sense something of the spirit of the Bard. Unscrupulous opportunists peddled anything that was linked to the dramatist, however remote or tenuous. David Garrick introduced the prestigious Shakespeare Festival in 1769 and by the early years of the nineteenth century there were around seven hundred annual visitors to the house. Shakespeare's birthplace, a picturesque town appropriately at the glorious heart of the English shires, was a tangible temple at which to worship the great man.

From the moment Shakespeare's birthplace opened its doors to the public, benefiting at last from official museum status, there has never been a noticeable lack of interest in this ancient building or its one-time occupant. Visitors – up to half a million a year – arrive in Henley Street from all parts of the world and for many it is an emotional pilgrimage. To step on this hallowed ground, often falling to their knees in reverence, is the fulfilment of a lifetime's ambition.

The opening of the house coincided with a period of great social upheaval. It was the middle of the nineteenth century and, with the advent of the railway age, Victorians were enjoying improved mobility and greater recreational freedom. The association with Dickens added prestige too, endorsing Shakespeare's Birthplace as the country's leading literary shrine.

Dickens was one of many eminent literary and theatrical figures who came to Stratford and inscribed their signature on a window that was originally at the front of the house. Sir Walter Scott, Thomas Carlyle, Mark Twain, Ellen Terry and Charlie Chaplin were among the distinguished visitors. Removed for safekeeping, the window can still be seen on the second floor of the house.

William Shakespeare 1564–1616

Anne Hathaway stayed at Stratford while her husband pursued a highly successful career in London as dramatist, actor and poet. Much of his life in the capital remains undocumented, though numerous scholars have speculated at length as to what precisely he did during those missing years. Many of Shakespeare's plays were not published in his lifetime but later earned him the reputation of the world's most celebrated dramatist and playwright. He is thought to have started writing plays around 1588, revising many for publication. He bought New Place, Stratford in 1597 and retired about 1613. The first collected edition of his works was published in 1623.

ARBURY HALL

GEORGE ELIOT'S EARLY LIFE was privileged and exclusive, but not as a result of wealth and position. Born Mary Ann Evans – she preferred Marian – her father, Robert, was land agent to Francis Newdigate, Viscount Daventry, owner of Grade I-listed Arbury Hall, an Elizabethan house remodelled in the Gothic style, and she spent her formative years on the estate. What she witnessed around her at that crucial early stage of her life was to provide her with a rich seam of material when she began writing *Scenes of Clerical Life*, consisting of three stories set in the same area. She was approaching forty by the time it was published. Later novels also drew on life at Arbury.

Mary Ann Evans was born at South Farm on the Arbury Estate. When she was about four months old, the family moved to nearby Griff House, where she lived until she was twenty. Her entire life revolved around this rural district of Warwickshire, only a stone's throw from the precise centre of England. During childhood, she would accompany her father to Arbury Hall, where he would leave her chatting to staff in the housekeeper's room. She was intrigued by the history of the house and the extensive Gothicizing, which took more than fifty years to complete. When the Newdigates were away she had free rein of the rooms and gradually came to know the house well. She also browsed in the library.

Robert Evans was a hard-working man whose duties on the estate were varied and wide-ranging. He collected rents, dealt with repairs, negotiated with road builders and surveyed land and buildings. Evans was respected for his honesty and integrity and his daughter later drew on his strength of character and admirable attitude to hard work for the eponymous hero of her first full-length novel, *Adam Bede*. Much of life in the Evans household when Marian was growing up was used as background material for *Middlemarch* and *Mill on the Floss*. Doricote Mill in the latter book is based on Griff House.

Arbury Hall was established as a monastery in the reign of Henry II. A casualty of the Dissolution, Arbury passed to Edmund Anderson, a lawyer, during the reign of Elizabeth I.

Then, as now, Arbury Hall and its 300-acre estate were largely cushioned from the real world and it is perhaps understandable that a novelist would find the place an endless source of fascination. If George Eliot were to return to Arbury today, she would still recognize it. In *Scenes of Clerical Life* she has created a minutely detailed working landscape consisting of a large country estate known as Cheverel Manor, a village called Shepperton and, at the heart of this rural district, a town by the name of Milby. Evans modelled these Warwickshire communities on the places that were an intricate part of her early life. What struck her most during those early years was the sharp contrast between the lives of the landed family at Arbury and those of its tenants.

Her memory was unusually accurate and acute; without the aid of notes and interviews with locals, she found she could recall people, places and events so strongly that the local inhabitants produced a key to her characters, identifying everyone except the author.

Evans was fascinated by Arbury Hall during the tenure of Sir Roger Newdigate, Francis's cousin, who was childless. It was he who instigated the lengthy Gothicizing of the house and became the model for Sir Christopher Cheverel. Sir Roger's second wife, Hester, is Lady Cheverel. Evans describes various architectural features of Cheverel Manor and, in Chapter 2 of 'Mr Gilfil's Love-Story' in *Scenes of Clerical Life*, the house is unmistakably Arbury Hall:

> Sir Christopher ... walked on to the eastern front of the building, where by the side of the grand entrance, was the large bow window of the saloon, opening on to the gravel sweep, and looking towards a long vista of undulating turf, bordered by tall trees, which, seeming to unite itself with the green of the meadows and a grassy road through a plantation, only terminated with the Gothic arch of a gateway in the far distance. The bow-window was open, and Sir Christopher, stepping in, found the group he sought, examining the progress of the unfinished ceiling.

The reference to the unfinished ceiling illustrates just how closely Evans has modelled Cheverel Manor on Arbury. In the story Sir

In *Scenes of Clerical Life*, George Eliot modelled Cheverel Manor on Arbury Hall. With its filigree tracery and pink-tinted glass, the saloon's projecting bow window is one of Arbury's most striking features.

Christopher Gothicizes Cheverel, just as Sir Roger transforms Arbury Hall in reality:

> The roads through the park were cut up by wagons carrying loads of stone from a neighbouring quarry, the green courtyard became dusty with lime, and the peaceful house rang with the sound of tools. For the next ten years Sir Christopher was occupied with the architectural metamorphosis of his old family mansion; thus anticipating, through the prompting of his individual taste, that general reaction from the insipid imitation of the Palladian style, towards a restoration of the Gothic, which marked the close of the eighteenth century.

Sir Christopher's desire to change Cheverel, watching it grow 'from ugliness into beauty', bordered on the obsessive, driven by 'that unswerving architectural purpose of his, conceived and carried out through long years of systematic personal execution, to something of the fervour of genius, as well as inflexibility of will'.

The Warwickshire influence of her childhood never left Marian Evans, although by the time she came to write *Felix Holt* in 1865, she regarded much of rural provincial England as a vanished world. The pace of life had accelerated, the railway age had dawned and a landscape once characterized by farms and market towns had been transformed by the rapid development of industry. In *Impressions of Theophrastus Such* (1879), her last published work, she describes her native county as 'fat central England'.

George Eliot 1819–80

Evans's early life at Arbury was blighted by the death of her beloved mother in 1836. She learnt German and Italian and she taught music, one of her great passions. Following her father's death in 1849, she travelled through Europe, returning to England the following year to begin writing for the *Westminster Review*. She mixed with other writers in eminent literary circles, one of whom was George Henry Lewes. In 1854 he and Evans entered into a relationship that would last until his death in 1878. However, Lewes, a biographer and editor, was married and unable to obtain a divorce so the couple lived together as man and wife, a somewhat unorthodox arrangement in straight-laced Victorian society. As a result, Evans became estranged from her family. Following the death of Lewes, Evans married John Walter Cross, a family friend for many years, in 1880.

Given the circumstances surrounding her relationship with Lewes and her growing reputation as a writer, she chose to adopt a pseudonym – that of George Eliot. Within ten years of meeting Lewes, she had written and published two of her best-known and most successful novels – *Adam Bede* (1859) and *The Mill on the Floss* (1860). Less familiar titles followed, including *Romola* (1863) before the final triumphs of *Middlemarch* (1871–2) and *Daniel Deronda* (1876).

Admired and commercially successful during her lifetime, Evans is regarded as one of the greatest Victorian writers, though her name faded somewhat in the years following her death. It was Virginia Woolf who restored Evans's reputation with an essay in *The Times Literary Supplement* in 1919, her centenary year. In it Woolf described *Middlemarch* as 'one of the very few English novels written for grown-up people'.

THE SAMUEL JOHNSON BIRTHPLACE MUSEUM

A portrait bust of Samuel Johnson created by the 18th century sculptor, Joseph Nollekens, a friend of the writer. However, Johnson considered the work to be less than flattering.

AT THE HEART OF the ancient city of Lichfield, located on the corner of Breadmarket Street and Market Street, is the house where Samuel Johnson was born and which, at the time of his birth, was his father Michael's bookshop. Johnson was delivered in the large room on the first floor of the house on 18 September 1709.

Three years earlier, Michael Johnson, an established Midlands bookseller, had borrowed heavily in order to acquire the entire library of the late Earl of Derby, which extended to nearly three thousand volumes. However, the scheme was not a success and many of the books remained unsold for years. Undeterred, Johnson moved on to another ambitious financial undertaking.

He bought a seventeenth-century house in Lichfield, a short distance from the parish church of St Mary and overlooking the Market Place. Johnson paid £80 for the house, which he immediately demolished and in its place built an imposing residence. His intention was to create a family home large enough to accommodate his bookselling business. The solid, four-storey house, which has changed little over the centuries, includes a basement and a second-hand bookshop on the ground floor. The top floor of the house would have been servants' and apprentices' quarters.

Samuel's parents' marriage suffered under the constant strain of his father's struggling business. There were demons driving him, too. Michael Johnson's doleful, melancholic nature cast a long shadow over the household and this obvious lack of warmth in the

The house where Samuel Johnson was born remained in his father Michael's possession for the rest of his life. Johnson senior intended to bequeath it to the people of Lichfield, but it was sold following his death for £235.

family led to young Samuel seeking consolation among the many books in his father's shop. He became an avid reader of tales of chivalry and romance and before he was ten years of age he was engrossed in the works of Shakespeare. At the age of nine he was reading *Hamlet* in the basement kitchen one day when he abruptly ran up the stairs to the street door. The ghost scene had greatly disturbed the youngster and he instinctively felt the urge to plunge back to normality and surround himself with people. By the time he went up to Oxford Johnson was widely read, although Shakespeare was a profound influence.

Following Michael Johnson's death in 1731, his widow ran the business until her own demise in 1759. Catherine Chambers, the family servant, then managed the shop. Little is known about the bookshop thereafter, although later tenants and owners included two booksellers. Over subsequent years the building operated as a newspaper office, a brazier's, a tinsmith's and a coffee shop. James Henry Johnson (no relation), anxious to save the premises from spoilers, bought the site for £800 in 1887. Following his death,

Lichfield City Council acquired Johnson's birthplace and officially opened it to the public in July 1901.

Classed as a biographical museum, charting Johnson's eventful journey through life, the Grade I-listed house includes many rare early editions of his work, as well as prints, paintings, manuscripts and items of furniture. So much of Johnson's birthplace is associated with books, crucially important in shaping and influencing the essayist and critic's life in the early years, and today serving as a permanent reminder of his skill and ability.

IZAAK WALTON'S COTTAGE

PASSENGERS ABOARD THE MANY trains that pass through the countryside between Stafford and Stoke-on-Trent may just catch a glimpse of a picturesque thatched cottage in a pretty garden surrounded by farmland a few yards from the line. The cottage lends

Izaak Walton's Cottage lies a few yards from a busy railway line. A spark from a passing steam train possibly started a major fire in the cottage's thatched roof in 1927. With its yew hedges and herbs, the garden is of particular interest to many visitors.

an air of rustic charm to the setting and most of those travellers who do spy it, albeit fleetingly, regard it no doubt as a perfect representation of a pastoral, chocolate-box England. As the cottage flashes past the window, however, many of those travellers would be unaware of its long history and its connection with one of Britain's most revered writers and countrymen.

Dating from the early seventeenth century, the half-timbered cottage belonged to Izaak Walton, who achieved literary status by writing *The Compleat Angler* in 1653. The cottage was part of Halfhead Farm, for which Walton paid £350. He took a keen interest in the business, which was managed by a tenant farmer. Walton was also a noted biographer, although ironically some of the details of his own life are somewhat sketchy. It is clear, however, that he never lived at the cottage and there is no evidence that he even set foot inside it.

He was a wealthy man; by the age of twenty-one he was running his own business as a linen merchant in Fleet Street. The success of

The interior of Izaak Walton's Cottage offers a fascinating insight into his many achievements. This manikin depicts the writer sitting at a table in the parlour.

155

his biography of the poet John Donne elevated him to the ranks of London's literati and, at the time of the English Civil War, he was a prosperous Staffordshire landowner. A farm labourer's cottage on an agricultural estate would have been far too humble a dwelling for a man of his means.

Walton, whose life spanned the reigns of four English monarchs, could never have envisaged how successful *The Compleat Angler* would become. After Shakespeare, the Bible and the Harry Potter series, this enduring guide to fishing and rural folklore is claimed to be the most published book in the English language and has never been out of print.

It was Walton's Royalist sympathies during the English Civil War that forced him to take a safe, neutral position in his choice of subject. Theological and political themes were completely out of the question. Instead, he chose the gentle pursuit of fishing, still one of Britain's most popular pastimes.

It may well have been Walton's writer friend Sir Henry Wotton, the Provost of Eton College, who introduced him to the delights of angling. Walton originally assisted Wotton by researching the life of

Izaak Walton's Cottage recalls his influence as an early conservationist. Standing by the inglenook fireplace in the scullery is a spinning wheel, one of a number of artefacts on display in the cottage.

John Donne for his forthcoming biography. However, Wotton died before the book was finished and Walton succeeded him as author. It is thought that the two men may have indulged in a little fishing on the Thames while discussing progress on the book. Walton later wrote a biography of Wotton.

Curiously, few of today's generation of anglers make their way to Izaak Walton's Cottage and those who do discover there is nothing to indicate what type of tackle he used when fishing. The general consensus among angling experts is that there was almost certainly no formal fishing equipment at that time. In all probability, Walton would have fashioned his rod from the branch of a tree and used a horsehair line. Until the Georgian era, fishing was a primitive, rudimentary business.

One of Walton's favourite rivers was the nearby Dove where he and his good friend Charles Cotton spent many days angling. Walton also fished the River Meon in Hampshire, reflecting that the picturesque valley 'exceeds all England for swift, shallow, clear, pleasant brooks and store of trout'.

The cottage remained part of Halfhead Farm until about 1920 when it was offered for sale on condition that the buyer opened it as a museum devoted to the memory of Izaak Walton. Local businessmen formed a trust and raised £50 to acquire the site. £500 was also needed to repair the dilapidated building. Lord Stafford performed the opening ceremony in 1924. However, improvements to the cottage were undone three years later when a fire swept through the thatched roof, possibly ignited by a spark from a passing steam train. The cottage was closed for a year.

A second, more extensive roof fire occurred in 1938 and yet again the cottage was closed for repair work, reopening the following year, with a safer, tiled roof to prevent further devastation. There are photographs inside the cottage of the opening ceremony. The trust was wound up in 1965, and Stafford Borough Council then acquired the cottage.

The garden is a delight and of great interest to many of the thousand or so annual visitors, characterized by old-fashioned roses, shrubs and herbaceous beds. There is also an extensive herb garden with a sweetly scented lavender hedge.

Today, the interior of the cottage illustrates the living and working conditions of a typical house of the seventeenth century. The history of angling through the centuries is also recorded. Although he never lived here, the cottage is synonymous with the name and reputation of a man whose love of the English countryside and knowledge of angling are immortalized in print.

Izaak Walton 1593–1683

Born in Stafford, Walton was the son of an alehouse keeper. Aged twenty-eight, he began work as an ironmonger in London and later married a great-grandniece of Thomas Cranmer. His second wife, Ann Ken, whom he married in 1647, was the half-sister of the hymn writer Thomas Ken. Walton counted eminent writers and clergymen among his circle of friends and he spent his latter years in Winchester. *Arte of Angling* (1577) was a valuable source of inspiration and ideas for Walton, who was encouraged to write about rods and lines and include descriptions of rivers and their fish stocks. In addition to *The Compleat Angler*, which was largely rewritten for the second edition, he wrote mainly biographies, including one of Richard Hooker, the English theologian. His study of John Donne appeared in 1640.

THE D.H. LAWRENCE BIRTHPLACE MUSEUM

NUMBER 8A VICTORIA STREET, Eastwood, eight miles to the west of Nottingham, has changed little since the Lawrence family lived here in the 1880s. This modest brick-built terraced house, a typical back-street dwelling of the period, where David Herbert (D.H.) Lawrence was born in the closing years of the Victorian era, demonstrates most effectively the humble living conditions and the social pecking order of the time.

Victoria Street was in an area of Eastwood known as the New Buildings. This took the form of a gridiron pattern of miners' cottages constructed by the local mining company in the 1850s. Today, the house is a museum – hence its close resemblance to the original family home – and from the moment you step inside it you gain a vivid impression of life in a Nottinghamshire mining

The miner's cottage, where the Lawrence family lived, and the immediate surroundings have been preserved to form part of a heritage industry devoted to the writer. The houses backed onto large common areas, which Lawrence later described as 'those sordid and hideous squares.'

community more than 125 years ago.

Lawrence's father, Arthur, was a coal miner at nearby Brinsley colliery, while his mother, Lydia, had been a teacher. The daughter of an engineer and Wesleyan lay preacher, Lydia was better educated than her husband, who let it be known that he loathed books. She was a woman of strong moral conviction and deeply religious. Like many women of the period, she had refined tastes and social aspirations. However, their time in Victoria Street was relatively short.

D.H. Lawrence was the fourth of five children and the youngest of three sons. He was known to his family as Bert. He was born in the upstairs front bedroom of the house, which is now part of the tour. The furniture and artefacts in this room (and throughout the museum) date from the Victorian period and there are several original items on display, including the bedside table, which belonged to Lydia.

D.H. Lawrence was born in the front bedroom at 8a Victoria Street. Limited resources meant that the bottom drawer of a chest in the room became a makeshift crib for the new baby.

With its sense of order, air of formality and square table and aspidistra as the centrepiece, the ground floor front parlour recalls the room least used in the house. Traditionally, in many of these houses, this was reserved for Sundays and special occasions, a tea-time visit from the local vicar perhaps, a family gathering or, inevitably, the laying out of a loved one in order that visitors could pay their respects. With the kitchen door opening to a yard providing access to the street and therefore in constant use, the front door was rarely opened, even though the outside step was regularly scrubbed. The state of the front step and the overall appearance of a house formed the yardstick by which the community judged and assessed its occupants.

The showpiece parlour has been recreated as the Lawrences would remember it. One original item of furniture remains; a chiffonier belonging to Lydia. In her case, the room also served as a shop window for the linen and baby clothes she made to produce a small income.

With its aspidistra, chiffonier and roaring fire, the front parlour was considered the best room in the house and rarely used.

Outside, at the back of the house, a washhouse also serves as a reminder of these long-forgotten, once bustling working-class communities. This was the era of the copper, the mangle and endless lines of washing beneath smoking chimneys and roofs of drab slate. The washhouse at 8a Victoria Street was communal and shared by three or four other families in the same terrace. Monday was designated washday, the longest and most arduous day of the week. There was always a great deal of work to do on this particular day – the volume was so great, in fact, that it was traditional for the family's eldest daughter to be kept off school in order to help.

My first visit to Eastwood, coinciding with the fiftieth anniversary of the famous Lady Chatterley trial in 2010, invited comparisons with a Lawrence novel. The autumn day was grey and gloomy, and heavy rain and winds lashed the little house of Lawrence's birth. The distant rooftops beyond Victoria Street glistened in the rain and the bleak greyness of the landscape that day brought to mind *Sons and Lovers*.

The people and places of Lawrence's childhood greatly influenced his writing. So much of Eastwood and this old industrial corner of Nottinghamshire is recreated in his work – in particular *Sons and Lovers*. The family left Victoria Street after two years and in 1891 they moved to a house in nearby Walker Street. Lawrence wrote: 'The scene of my Nottinghamshire–Derbyshire novels all centres round Eastwood where I was born: and whoever stands on Walker Street will see the whole landscape of *Sons and Lovers* before him.'

D.H. Lawrence 1885–1930

When he was born, Lawrence was a sickly baby with a weak chest and it was feared he wouldn't survive. Poor health plagued him all his life, compounded by several bouts of pneumonia. Other children at school regarded him as a weakling and he certainly wasn't robust enough to play football or other rough games. Consequently he was drawn to the girls in the classroom and the playground.

Lawrence spent his formative years in Eastwood, his working-class background as the son of a miner giving him an extraordinary insight into the human condition and the layered structure of the class system. With his mother's encouragement he became a schoolmaster and, following the success of his first novel *The White Peacock* (1911), he became a full-time novelist and poet. A year later he eloped with Frieda Weekley, the wife of his former professor at Nottingham University. They married in 1914 after her divorce and following the publication of *Sons and Lovers*, his semi-autobiographical and most popular novel, a year earlier. Struggling to make ends meet, the Lawrences lived a peripatetic, nomadic existence, residing at numerous different addresses courtesy of friends and travelling extensively in Europe.

D.H. Lawrence died of tuberculosis. Thirty years after his death his infamous novel *Lady Chatterley's Lover* (1928) drew a new generation of readers after a High Court judgment permitted Penguin Books to publish an unexpurgated edition of the book. The novel's sexually explicit subject matter remains the subject of debate (although by today's standards it seems tame, almost commonplace).

NEWSTEAD ABBEY

I⊤ COULD BE ARGUED that Newstead Abbey's eventful past is no less fascinating than the short but extraordinary life of its most famous occupant, George Gordon, 6th Lord Byron, who resided at Newstead between 1808 and 1814. His tenure here was brief but it represents an especially colourful chapter in the story of this famous ancient building.

Newstead Abbey, the former home of the Romantic poet George Gordon, 6th Lord Byron. On the left is the West Front of the old priory church, dating back to 1274 and damaged during the Civil War.

Overlooking lakes and 300 acres of parkland and gardens, Newstead was founded by Henry II as an Augustinian Priory in the twelfth century. Over the years there has been speculation as to the reason for its foundation. Officially, Henry established Newstead in memory of his grandfather, but there is also a suggestion that the decision was made in atonement for the murder of Thomas Becket. Following the Dissolution, Newstead passed to Sir John Byron, or 'Little Sir John of the Great Beard' as he was known.

Sir John subsequently converted Newstead into an imposing family residence and the estate remained the principal country seat of the Byrons for nearly three hundred years. One of Sir John's descendants, the 5th Lord Byron, known as the 'Wicked Lord', lived there as a recluse. He is known to have killed his cousin in a duel. He died eventually in the scullery, apparently the only part of the house with a watertight roof. After his death, the house passed to his great-nephew, George Byron, the renowned poet.

Byron was ten years old when he inherited Newstead Abbey in 1798. However, the young heir was in for an unpleasant surprise. Arriving in Nottinghamshire with his mother, he discovered the house to be in a near-ruinous state. Byron found the Great Hall had been stripped of everything, including the fireplace, to help pay creditors and elsewhere there were countless examples of the effects of dereliction and decay. His great-uncle had, in effect, passed him a poisoned chalice. However, the scale of the estate appealed to Byron's sense of showmanship and the grandiose and, although he never lived permanently at Newstead, he visited this noted romantic ruin many times over the years.

The plaster bust in the window bay on the Grand Staircase is a portrait of Byron by the sculptor E.H. Bailey. The bust is dated 1826.

Lack of money meant Bryon was unable to transform Newstead Abbey as he would have wished, but his time there was extravagantly occupied in other ways. He was never boring and his flamboyant style and extraordinarily colourful imagination led him to live the life of a true eccentric while at Newstead. In addition to hosting wild parties, he indulged in pistol practice in the Great Hall, boxed in the drawing room and allowed a tame bear and a wolf to roam the corridors.

Although finances were tight, he did manage to acquire enough cash to refurbish two apartments – one for his mother and one for himself. Once the work was finished, typically, he staged a lavish party for his friends. He and his guests stayed in bed until the middle of the day and then spent the remainder of it fencing, riding, playing cricket and sailing on the lakes. In keeping with Byron's taste for the absurd, the evening's entertainment demanded the party-goers dress as monks.

There was also a strict code at Newstead regarding servants. Byron only employed staff whose features were perfectly formed

The Upper Lake at Newstead Abbey, where Byron swam with his dogs, Boatswain and Lyon. The fort is one of several structures constructed by the 5th Lord Byron, which he used for mock battles on the lake.

and exquisite to the eye. Anyone who was in any way ugly or flawed was dismissed without question. It seems that earlier generations of Byrons were equally unconventional and capricious in their behaviour. Servants were also ordered to take part in military exercises on the lakes at Newstead, fighting across the water in miniature battleships with the use of live ammunition.

On Newstead's first floor, leading off the Great Hall, is Byron's splendid, oak-panelled dining room The late eighteenth-century Hepplewhite dining furniture is strikingly similar to the original items found here. The splendid carved, heraldic overmantle came from Colwick Hall, a nearby Byron property and bears the date 1556, as well as the family crest and Latin motto *Crede Byron* (Trust in Byron).

A spiral staircase leads to Byron's bedroom and dressing room, greatly altered since he lived there. He brought the four-poster bed, with its domed canopy and gilded tester with four baron's coronets, from his undergraduate rooms at Trinity College, Cambridge and always slept with loaded pistols near him. Every day, he ensured they were in good working order.

The adjoining dressing room was stripped out in 1814 in readiness for redecoration, but never restored. This room is one of Newstead's most fascinating and atmospheric features, not least because it is reputed to be haunted. Byron claimed to have been visited here in 1814 by the ghost of a monk who warned him not to marry Annabella Milbanke. Typically, it was advice that the arrogant Byron did not heed. The marriage went ahead but did not last. The ghost of the monk inspired the black friar in the Norman abbey in Byron's masterly satire *Don Juan*.

Byron's impecunious position eventually forced him to quit Newstead Abbey in order to meet massive rising debts. He sold the former mediaeval priory to his friend Thomas Wildman who had inherited a fortune from plantations owned by his family in Jamaica. The sale price of £94,500 was agreed in 1818 and Newstead remained the Wildman home for the next forty years, during which time it was transformed into the late-Georgian, early-Victorian Norman and Gothic style.

Following Wildman's death in 1859, Newstead was bought by

William Frederick Webb, an affluent landowner. The new owner was a friend of the explorer David Livingstone who had saved Webb's life in Africa. Livingstone stayed at Newstead as Webb's guest.

Webb and his descendants owned Newstead until the early years of the twentieth century; in 1931 it passed to Nottingham Corporation, which now maintains it as a museum.

George Gordon, Lord Byron 1788–1824

Byron was born in London. His grandfather was a naval officer and his parents were Captain 'Mad Jack' Byron and Catherine Gordon of Gight, Aberdeen, a Scottish heiress. His mother's violent nature and his own physical disability – he was lame from birth – may account for Byron's flamboyant style, curious actions and wayward behaviour in later life. In 1798 he succeeded to the title of 6th Baron of Rochdale on the death of his great-uncle. Byron was educated at Aberdeen Grammar School, then privately at Dulwich and at Harrow. He attended Trinity College, Cambridge, in 1805 where he led a dissolute life. An early collection of poems, *Hours of Idleness*, was poorly received and Byron set off on a grand tour, which took him to Spain, Malta, Greece and Albania, among other destinations. His travels were described in *Childe Harold's Pilgrimage* (1812–18).

Following the publication of the first two cantos, Byron found fame overnight and was soon acknowledged as one of the most celebrated public figures of his day – the equivalent of a major celebrity in today's world. His status and notoriety were further consolidated when he began an affair with Lady Caroline Lamb, which became the subject of considerable national interest. He married Anne Isabella Milbanke in 1815; she left him a year later after the birth of their daughter, Ada. There were also rumours that he enjoyed an incestuous relationship with his half-sister, Augusta Leigh. Shunned by society, Byron fled to Europe once more and met Shelley. In Venice he met Teresa Guiccioli, who became his mistress. Some of the poet's best work dates from this period, including *Beppo* (1818), *A Vision of Judgment* (1822) and the satirical *Don Juan* (1819–24).

Byron died of marsh fever at Missolonghi, having joined the Greek insurgents who had risen against the Turks. His remains were brought back to England and buried at Hucknall Torkard, near Newstead Abbey.

RENISHAW HALL

DURING THE MIDDLE TO latter half of the 1960s a young girl aged between five and ten could often be found playing contentedly in the expansive grounds of Renishaw Hall. It was hardly an unusual spectacle and the child was simply doing what all children love to do. On her first foray into the great outdoors, however, Alexandra Sitwell, who grew up to be the present chatelaine of Renishaw Hall, was perhaps a little surprised to find her boots coated in coal dust, an inevitable consequence of living in an industrial landscape, which it remained until the 1980s when the nearby Renishaw Park Colliery finally closed.

The Sitwells could hardly complain. They had made their money from industry. Before the discovery of a rich seam of coal on the estate, they were the largest manufacturers of iron nails in the world, a combination of hard graft and good fortune affording them the trappings of success.

Not long before the young Alexandra Sitwell discovered coal dust on her boots while out playing one day, she and her parents had arrived at Renishaw Hall by car from London. The year was 1965 but this was no ordinary day. As they journeyed up the long drive to the house, Alexandra shut her eyes, the sense of excitement and anticipation almost overwhelming. The seven-year-old child was about to discover Renishaw Hall.

Her father, Sir Reresby Sitwell, had just inherited the Renishaw Estate from his uncle, Osbert Sitwell. In those days the house was cold and damp in winter, much of it little used throughout the year. Often, on freezing, frosty mornings, the temperature was so low in the house that the family would retreat to the warmth and comfort of their car after breakfast to read the morning papers.

As she grew up, Alexandra often pondered on the history of Renishaw Hall, the Sitwell lineage and the family's impressive literary legacy. The Sitwells were not aristocrats; rather, they were responsible landowners and eccentric socialites.

Even today, their name alone recalls the renowned quirkiness of this celebrated family.

The home of the Sitwell family for over 350 years, Renishaw

The Sitwells made their money from nails and coal and the house is testament to their success.

Hall was built for George Sitwell, High Sheriff of Derbyshire, in 1625. It was originally a modest manor house in the Pennine style, with later additions and alterations. The influence of Edwin Lutyens is also evident. The interior includes an eclectic mix of furniture and artefacts, with many pieces added by subsequent generations of the Sitwell family. The house also contains in the region of thirty thousand books.

Around the beginning of the twentieth century, almost a hundred years before the closure of Renishaw Park Colliery, another generation of Sitwell children played in the grounds of Renishaw Hall. Edith and her two younger brothers, Osbert and Sacheverell – Alexandra Sitwell's great-aunt, great-uncle and grandfather – were an inseparable trio, playing and acting out their fantasies in the vast house and garden.

The children tended to spend more time with the servants than with their ill-matched parents. The Sitwells' butler, Henry Moat, was a particularly close ally, warning them if their father, Sir George Sitwell, was approaching. Edith's relationship with Sir George and

The Sitwell children, Edith, Osbert and Sacheverell, played happily in the garden at Renishaw Hall. Their biographer, Anthony Powell, described them as 'style-setters ... heroes to a new generation of dandy writers.'

her mother was distant and strained. It was hardly surprising, given that her parents had wished for a boy.

In adulthood the Sitwell siblings moved to London, although they returned regularly to Renishaw. By the 1920s they were established members of London's celebrated literary society, with Sacheverell the most prolific of the Sitwell writers. A typical day at Renishaw would begin with Edith writing copiously in her notebooks from her four-poster bed, which can still be seen at the Grade I-listed house. Edith's biographer, Sarah Bradford, describes the writer as: '[lying] late in bed in a bedroom heavy with the scent of discarded gardenias and tuberoses, reading French novels, newspapers or letters, or playing Patience on a flat-folding leather card-tray.'

Edith was deeply attached to the childhood home from which she drew her inspiration, and although she lived mostly in London, her spirit was at Renishaw. She loved the grandeur of the house, its atmosphere and air of solitude.

Between the wars, when the Sitwell writers were at their most influential, Renishaw played host to countless visitors of note.

Evelyn Waugh was a regular guest who believed that the Sitwells 'took the dullness out of literature', and William Walton visited on occasions. There are photographs of him as a young man at Renishaw. Highly eccentric, idiosyncratic and very much at the centre of their own world, the Sitwells worked hard but they also lived well and enjoyed a lavish lifestyle. Their output was vast – almost two hundred volumes of poetry, fiction, biography, music, art and literary criticism.

During the Second World War, against a background of nightly air raids and constant uncertainty, Edith and Osbert fled London, retreating to Renishaw Hall where they would write in the soft light of oil lamps. Edith also spent much of her time knitting for army friends; among them the actor Alec Guinness, for whom she produced a pair of seaboot stockings.

None of the Sitwells was at home when D.H. Lawrence, on a rare visit to his native Midlands, called at Renishaw Hall one day in September 1926. In his book *Façades – the life of the Sitwells*, John Pearson writes: 'The house was closed and Lawrence ... was left with an impression of Renishaw at its most unwelcoming. He would never forget it.' Lawrence finally met Osbert and Edith in Tuscany the following spring. It was the only time they would meet.

A month or so after the visit to Renishaw, Lawrence began work on the first draft of *Lady Chatterley's Lover*. In the story Wragby Hall, home of the Chatterleys, is described as 'a long low old house in brown stone, begun about the middle of the eighteenth century and added onto, till it was a warren of a place without much distinction'. Wragby Hall may have been influenced by Lawrence's visit to Renishaw, although the Sitwell family seat is some 125 years older. However, Wragby's position in the shadow of the Derbyshire coalfield fits with the setting. A reference to Lady Chatterley travelling to nearby Chesterfield adds credence to the theory. Lawrence may even have based the Chatterley family on the Sitwells. Not surprisingly, Edith later condemned *Lady Chatterley's Lover* as 'a dirty and worthless book'.

Edith Sitwell 1887–1964

Born in Scarborough, Edith was the eldest of the Sitwells. Her father, George, was MP for the Yorkshire seaside town. An unhappy child, life at Renishaw Hall was made more bearable by the company of her two brothers and the encouragement of a governess, who introduced the young Edith to music and literature. Much of her poetry written between the two World Wars denounces the cruelty of man, justified by the Second World War and the dropping of the atom bomb. Her first volume of poetry *Façade*, written in 1923 and declaimed to music by Sir William Walton, caught the public's attention when it was given a controversial reading in London. Other works include *Elegy for Dead Fashion* (1926) and *Fanfare of Elizabeth* (1946). In her heyday, Edith Sitwell led a colourful, rewarding life, mingling with the Hollywood set and taking tea with Marilyn Monroe. She was made a Dame of the British Empire in 1954. Immensely tall, with an oval face and aquiline nose, her appearance was somewhat alarming, though her endearing, flamboyant personality shone through. She was witty and amusing and unfailingly loyal to her friends.

Osbert (Francis) Sitwell 1892–1969

Born in London, Osbert was educated at Eton and raised at Renishaw Hall, which he later inherited. Reluctantly, he served in the Great War and his pacifist views are reflected in his early satirical poetry. Among his publications are a series of travel books, several novels and a five-volume autobiography, *Left Hand: Right Hand*.

Sacheverell Sitwell 1897–1988

Sacheverell was educated at Eton before becoming an officer in the Grenadier Guards. He later became a prolific writer, best known for his acclaimed travel books. He also published poetry, was a renowned art critic and raconteur and wrote biographies of Mozart (1932) and Liszt (1934).

THE EAST OF ENGLAND

THE MANOR, HEMINGFORD GREY

THE MANOR AT HEMINGFORD GREY is one of England's oldest houses. Begun by the Normans around 1130, it survives as a fascinating relic of the distant past. Despite alterations and a fire in the late eighteenth century, most of the original structure remains. At first glance, its long history and pedigree suggest it is an ecclesiastical building or some form of ruin, its ancient walls adorned with information panels and illustrations telling its story and pointing to the different stages of its development. This could not be further from the truth. The house has been continuously occupied for nearly nine hundred years, but very little is written about it and, although it is open to the public, it is essentially a home, not a museum.

The Manor is a secret place, just yards from the River Ouse and only a stone's throw from the town of Huntingdon. Entering through the little gate from the riverbank, visitors are immediately struck by its romantic setting and tangible sense of history. The thick stone walls and Norman features seem to hide dark mysteries. The house has weathered the centuries of social and political upheaval but it remains a place where the imagination is irresistibly stirred.

It seems apt, therefore, that for many years this was the home of the writer Lucy Boston who bought the house just before the outbreak of the Second World War. Boston first saw the Manor from the river in 1915 and thought it looked tranquil, though unloved. She thought of the house often in the intervening years and then, when her marriage collapsed and she was looking for a home, she learnt there was a property for sale in the village of Hemingford

It was from this stretch of the River Ouse, during the early stages of the First World War, that Lucy Boston spotted the Manor at Hemingford Grey. Villagers were wary of walking along the towpath beside the Manor, believing the house to be haunted.

When Lucy Boston bought the Manor, the house was poor condition, with much of its original structure concealed by later Georgian additions. Boston's painstaking restoration of the house took several years to complete.

174

Grey. It was the late 1930s and Boston was renting a flat in Cambridge some fourteen miles away. She leapt into a taxi and came straight to the village. Without hesitation Boston went ahead and bought the Manor, becoming its latest occupant on 31 May, 1939. For the next fifty years she dedicated much of her time at the house to its preservation and restoration.

At the time she bought the house, the garden was little more than a couple of fields. Boston soon changed that, planting yew trees, which she later redesigned as topiary, and cultivating old roses. She was an especially creative and resourceful woman who could turn her hand to many things. However, she soon aroused suspicion in the neighbourhood. It was wartime and a woman living alone in a large house was always going to be a prime suspect for treason.

In Lucy Boston's case, the locals felt they had good reason to fear they had a traitor in their midst. Astute locals in Hemingford Grey apparently discovered that Boston could speak German and that before the war she had worked as an artist in Italy and Austria. Was she a spy? Concern in the village grew when it became apparent she had left the Manor's attic light burning on several occasions, despite the blackout regulations. People immediately believed she was signalling to enemy forces, no doubt acquiring vital information from any one of the local RAF stations.

Boston did indeed have links with the local military in this corner of East Anglia, but her motives were harmless and entirely patriotic. In the early years of the war she invited servicemen, based in the area, to attend regular concerts of classical music played on her 1929 gramophone. The concerts were held twice a week in the music room at the Manor and they proved so popular that additional seating, in the form of a mattress and the back seats of Boston's car, was provided.

After the war a sense of calm enveloped the Manor once again, although life was very different. Against the grey austerity of the early 1950s Lucy Boston turned her attention to writing, imagining her wonderful old home and its garden as the backdrop for many of her stories. Her first book *Yew Hall*, a novel for adults, was published in 1954. The plot deals with dark themes, including murder and suicide, and the setting is a country house with an air of creeping malevolence.

The same year saw the publication of her first children's book *The Children of Green Knowe*, the first in a series of six titles in which the Manor and its four-acre garden become the setting for an ancient, haunted house deep in the country. Mostly, the books are time-travel fantasies, unlocking secrets of Green Knowe's past and introducing the reader to children who were acquainted with the house in previous centuries. With its evocative writing and inspired storytelling, the Green Knowe series is acknowledged as one of the greatest achievements in contemporary children's literature. Boston's son Peter illustrated the books and several striking examples of his work can be seen on the tour of the Manor.

In the first book, a young boy named Toseland (Tolly) goes to live with his great-grandmother, Mrs Oldknow, at her isolated home beside a river. So begins an incredible journey into a world of myth and fantasy, a wonderland of snowy winter wastes, surreal supernatural images and quirky nooks and crannies. Interestingly, Boston borrowed the name Oldknow from an American airman attending one of her gramophone recitals. She later sent him a copy of the book in gratitude.

Visiting the Manor confirms its place in the Green Knowe stories, offering 'a unique opportunity to walk into the books', as the marketing blurb says. Children, discovering a veritable treasure trove, complete with rocking horse and toy box, gaze at the house in wide-eyed amazement, seeing all around them what their boundless imagination has dictated.

The Manor's present occupant, Lucy Boston's daughter-in-law Diana, who conducts tours of the house and garden, sets the scene when visitors knock on the door by explaining the circumstances surrounding Tolly's arrival at Green Knowe. In 1947, eight years after Boston moved to the house, winter floods overwhelmed much of East Anglia. The author was marooned at the Manor for over a week as the floodwater did its best to breach the threshold. However, the experience proved to be unexpectedly fruitful. In the opening chapter of *The Children of Green Knowe*, Tolly journeys by train and taxi through a desolate flooded landscape. He eventually arrives at the house by boat, rowing up to the front door by the light of a lantern:

> Mr Boggis [the gardener] handed him the lantern and told him to kneel up in the bows with it and shout if they were likely to bump into anything. They rowed round two corners in the road and then in at a big white gate. Toseland waved the lantern about and saw trees and bushes in the water, and presently the boat was rocked by quite a strong current and the reflection of the lantern streamed away in elastic jigsaw shapes and made gold rings round the tree trunks. At last they came to a still pool reaching the steps of the house, and the keel of the boat grated on gravel. The windows were all lit up, but it was too dark to see what kind of a house it was, only that it was high and narrow like a tower.

Reading the stories, it comes as no surprise to discover the house, to which, for more than half a century, she devoted so much of her time and energy, lies at the heart of the Green Knowe series. Boston's beloved Manor was her inspiration and the driving force behind her writing.

Lucy M. Boston 1892–1990

Lucy Boston was the fifth of six children and her father was an engineer and sometime mayor of Southport on the Lancashire coast where she was born. She undertook voluntary nursing during the First World War and married William Boston, a distant cousin, in 1917. Their only son, Peter, was born a year later. The marriage ended in the mid-1930s and she spent several years working in Europe until the threat of war drove her back to Britain where she settled in East Anglia. Boston gradually restored her new home, the Manor at Hemingford Grey, near Huntingdon, and it was at the house between 1954 and 1961 that she wrote the Green Knowe stories. Other books include *The Castle of Yew* (1965), a collection of poems, *Time is Undone* (1977), and two volumes of autobiography, *Memory in a House* (1973) and *Perverse and Foolish* (1979). Lucy Boston was a woman of immense energy and stamina; she was outspoken, fiercely independent and fearless. She lived into advanced old age and is buried in the adjoining village of Hemingford Abbots.

SHAW'S CORNER

DURING THE DARK, UNCERTAIN days of the First World War, the residents of a sleepy Hertfordshire village viewed the rather strange middle-aged man who lived at the former rectory with a certain unease and suspicion. He kept a light burning in a window at the top of the house and he was distinctly odd – 'a rum one, a very rum one'. Could they have a spy, a traitor in their midst?

The people of Ayot St Lawrence knew this man was a writer but his literary credentials didn't interest or impress them. They knew him to be the celebrated Irish playwright George Bernard Shaw and that was really all they needed to know. By the time the Great War began, Shaw and his wife Charlotte had lived at the New Rectory, built in 1902, for eight years, though the great man was rarely seen in the village. The couple would remain at the house for the rest of their lives, the widowed Shaw dying there in advanced old age.

The Shaws chose Ayot St Lawrence for its rural setting and close proximity to London, although the house itself was not to their liking and initially they didn't plan to make it their permanent home. When the couple viewed it, it was still in use as the parish rectory, although the present incumbent was struggling to afford to live there. The Shaws chose to rent the house, believing it to be a short-term answer to finding a suitable property in the area. As it turned out, they continued with this arrangement for a total of fourteen years, eventually buying the house, which then became known as Shaw's Corner, two years after the end of the First World War.

The twelfth-century village of Ayot St Lawrence, barely touched by the passage of time when the Shaws moved there in 1906, had two churches and one shop but no bus or train service and no water, gas or electricity supply. Unlike most of the villagers, the Shaws were able to use a private electrical generating plant for their power. The house itself stood in a sloping 3½-acre plot with a kitchen garden, orchard, lawn and a belt of conifers. Inside Shaw's Corner were a dining room, small drawing room and eight bedrooms.

There was also a study in the house, although Shaw spent many happy, waking hours writing in his small hut in the garden. Visitors to Shaw's Corner often mistook the hut for a tool shed from the outside, but stepping inside confirmed this was Shaw's precious sanctuary where he could think and write without noise and interruption.

The hut's revolving base allowed Shaw to follow the sun. The writer would simply lean his shoulder against the structure when necessary and the hut would shift to the appropriate position. An electric stove provided heat in the winter and a telephone connected him to the rest of the world. It was in this quaint little hut, in a spacious garden in the middle of the English Home Counties, that George Bernard Shaw produced some of his best-known work. His typewriter, spectacles and notebooks can still be seen inside the hut.

The villagers' distrust of Shaw was compounded by the publication of his highly controversial and inflammatory anti-war pamphlet 'Common Sense about the War' (1914). There were threats of violence, and invitations to speak in public were suddenly withdrawn or declined. However, it was an Act of God, not the man-made consequences of war, that finally redeemed him in the eyes of his neighbours.

In 1915, following the devastating effects of what became known as the Hertfordshire Blizzard, Shaw joined fellow villagers and country dwellers to clear the roads of fallen trees and other debris. It was a rare natural disaster and the damage was widespread. The menfolk of Ayot St Lawrence, including Shaw, joined together with one common aim. That same year, Shaw would have been reminded of the futility of war when a German Zeppelin floated over the house one evening, crashing in a nearby field.

A quarter of a century later England was a country once again embroiled in war. By now George Bernard Shaw was eighty-four, although age had not dimmed him or dented his faculties; far from it. He was spry and active in old age and could often be found chopping wood, lighting bonfires, sawing logs or collecting acorns. He was a keen hiker too, often walking up to six miles a day and instantly recognizable in his knee breeches, wide-brimmed hat and Norfolk jacket. In addition to physical tasks and regular exercise, Shaw spent much of his time dictating letters to fellow socialists, actors and directors. He continued to drive, although his chauffeur sat nervously alongside him in the front of the car, guiding his employer through the controls when necessary.

Life at Shaw's Corner during this critical period was not without a touch of glamour. Hollywood actor and singer Danny Kaye visited the house, as did the beautiful but emotionally fragile British actress Vivien Leigh, who came to Ayot St Lawrence in 1944 when she was at the height of her fame. The star of *Gone with the Wind*, produced in Hollywood five years earlier, had agreed to appear in J. Arthur Rank's film adaptation of *Caesar and Cleopatra*, written by Shaw in 1901. The playwright had never met Leigh and he was anxious to satisfy himself that she was suitable to play the beauty of the Nile. Accompanied by the Hungarian director Gabriel Pascal, Leigh walked in the garden and visited the hut. The film went ahead with her in the starring role. Another reminder of Shaw's cinematic success is his Oscar for the film version of *Pygmalion*, made in 1938. The gold statuette is on display in the house.

A year before Vivien Leigh's visit, Shaw had lost Charlotte to a chronic bone disease and by now he himself was entering the last phase of a long and eventful life. He died at Shaw's Corner aged

The gate at Shaw's Corner. In the garden beyond, Shaw's ashes were scattered following his death from renal failure in 1950.

ninety-four, after falling from an apple tree he was attempting to prune, and his ashes, together with those of his wife, were scattered in the garden and around the statue of Saint Joan. Today, the Arts and Crafts villa remains much as it was when it was the country home of one of Ireland's greatest dramatists.

George Bernard Shaw 1856–1950

Born in Dublin, Shaw was the youngest child of Irish Protestant parents. His father was a grain merchant and civil servant. Aged twenty, Shaw moved to London and worked as a journalist. A devout socialist, he became drama critic of the *Saturday Review* (1895–98) and later joined the newly established Fabian Society. At the turn of the century he entered the arena of local politics, serving as a councillor for St Pancras (1897–1903).

Between 1879 and 1883 he had written five novels, all of which were rejected but later published, and his first play, *Widowers' Houses*, produced in 1892, made little impact. However, his subsequent work was largely successful, and included *The Devil's Disciple*, (1897), *Mrs Warren's Profession* (1898), *Man and Superman* (1902) and *Major Barbara* (1905). *The Apple Cart* (1929), which has been regularly staged over the years, and *Too Good to be True* (1932) are among many plays written at Shaw's Corner. He wrote over sixty plays in all, many of them still performed throughout the world. Shaw received the Nobel Prize for Literature in 1925.

THE NORTH OF ENGLAND

ELIZABETH GASKELL'S HOUSE

ELIZABETH GASKELL AND HER husband William moved to 84 Plymouth Grove in June 1850, following the publication of her first novel *Mary Barton* two years earlier. The house was Gaskell's permanent home for the remaining fifteen years of her life and although she was happy there, the tone and wording of some of her letters tell a different story. During that period she became fretful, distracted and self-analytical.

The year of the move to Plymouth Grove, Gaskell wrote to her friend Eliza Fox:

> We've got a house. ... And if I had neither conscience nor prudence I should be delighted, for it certainly is a beauty. ... You *must* come and see us in it, dearest Tottie, and make me see 'the wrong the better cause' and that it is right to spend so much ourselves on *so* purely a selfish thing as a house is, while so many are wanting.

Gaskell's social conscience and her concern for the plight of the less fortunate led her to question the moral value of acquiring such a sizeable house as well as the viability of running a property on this scale. The rent alone was £150 per year, roughly half her husband's annual income as a Unitarian minister. Gaskell wrote: 'My dear! It's £150 a year, and I dare say we shall be ruined; and I've already asked after the ventilation of the new Borough Gaol.'

However, Gaskell's subsequent increased success as a novelist rescued the situation. In the last years of her life she was paid handsomely to write a biography of Charlotte Brontë and for the serialization of her own novel *Wives and Daughters* (1865).

Plymouth Grove lies a couple of miles from the centre of Manchester, in the suburb of Ardwick. The large Grade II*-listed, seven-bedroom house dates back to the late 1830s and, with its Italianate double-fronted design, it remains one of very few surviving Regency-style villas in the city. Gaskell's two previous homes in Manchester have long gone.

The size and scale of Plymouth Grove allowed Gaskell to entertain her many friends and social contacts in comfort and it was here that she wrote two of her best-known novels, *Cranford* (1853) and *North and South* (1855). Outside in the garden she sketched in additional detail by introducing plants and domestic animals. A pigsty was built and soon a cow, hens and pretty white ducks could be seen in the grounds of the novelist's home.

Charlotte Brontë visited Plymouth Grove on a number of occasions between 1851 and 1854, describing it as 'a large, cheerful, airy

The Italianate stucco house in Plymouth Grove includes a striking portico. Elizabeth Gaskell's desk in the front hall was positioned so that she could see the garden, children, servants and front door from where she sat.

house, quite out of Manchester smoke'. The smoke to which Brontë referred was smog that emanated from the textile factories and cotton mills in the newly industrialized areas of the city, specifically Ancoats. By the middle of the nineteenth century, there were more than a hundred mills in Manchester.

Brontë was shy and reclusive and it is claimed that on one of her visits to the house, she hid behind the curtains in the drawing room in order to avoid contact with other visitors. Dickens, visiting Manchester in September 1852 to speak at the opening of the city's Central Library, called at the house unexpectedly at 10 a.m. Gaskell thought the time of his arrival to be 'far too early'.

Other notable visitors to the house included John Ruskin, the American writer Charles Eliot Norton and the conductor Charles Hallé, who taught Gaskell's daughter Meta to play the piano. It was a busy household and, according to Barbara Brill, William Gaskell's biographer, 'Plymouth Grove could be likened to the activities of a beehive.'

Gaskell's husband survived her by almost twenty years and, following his death, his two unmarried daughters, Julia and Meta, continued to live in the house until their deaths in 1908 and 1913 respectively. Meta's passing marked the end of the Gaskell family's unbroken sixty-year occupancy of Plymouth Grove.

Following Meta's death, the future of Plymouth Grove seemed uncertain. Pressure grew to open the house as a museum dedicated to the memory of Elizabeth Gaskell and her literary achievements, a concept supported by the *Manchester Guardian*. However, the local authority rejected the plan on the grounds that: 'The house belonged to one of the ugliest periods of architecture and was of no value beyond its association with the Gaskell family.'

Many years passed before the University of Manchester acquired the redundant house in 1969, adapting it for use by the International Society. The Manchester Historic Buildings Trust acquired the freehold in 2004. By then the Grade II*-listed house was in a poor state and on the English Heritage Buildings at Risk Register. The Trust first repaired the roof; then by 2014 had raised sufficient funds to complete the restoration of the entire property.

Plymouth Grove and its garden have now been transformed to

reflect the Gaskell family home as members of its household would have known it. Surviving items, including Gaskell's wedding veil and passport, are complemented by authentic nineteenth-century furniture, giving a revealing insight into the life and cherished home of one of the nineteenth century's most readable and admired novelists.

Elizabeth Gaskell 1810–65

The daughter of a Unitarian preacher, Elizabeth Gaskell spent her formative years with an aunt in the Cheshire town of Knutsford. Her mother had died when she was an infant. Gaskell based *Cranford* on her 'dear, adopted native town'. Her love of Knutsford and its people is apparent in her writing and the book's detailed study of women's lives in a small country town has been closely scrutinized by feminist critics over the years. Gaskell's first novel *Mary Barton* (1848) greatly impressed Dickens who published much of her work in his *Household Words*. *Ruth* (1853) was a controversial piece of fiction, dealing with the social stigma of illegitimacy, and her noted humanitarianism significantly influenced what came to be known as the 'Condition of England' novel. Elizabeth Gaskell bore six children and died suddenly of heart failure aged fifty-five.

THE PARSONAGE, HAWORTH

A LOW BANK OF cloud lay above me, darkening the rows of gritstone houses and the bleak Pennine moorland surrounding them. A dank, misty morning in autumn or winter is perhaps the ideal time to visit the West Yorkshire home of the Brontës, the atmosphere and mood of the setting perfectly capturing the spirit of this extraordinary trio of writers, still loved and adored throughout the world. Summer is always busy at the parsonage, and the sheer number of tourists who stream through the Georgian house and throng Haworth's steep village street, with its lines of tearooms and souvenir shops, can sometimes dilute the magic.

The Brontës came to Haworth in 1820 following Patrick Brontë's appointment as perpetual curate of the parish church. The village was a very different place in the early years of the nineteenth

'Haworth expresses the Brontës; the Brontës express Haworth,' wrote Virginia Woolf after a visit to the parsonage early in the twentieth century. 'They fit like a snail to its shell.'

century. This was a remote, manufacturing community where daily life was a constant struggle and there was considerable poverty and hardship. There was no proper sanitation and many villagers lived in appalling, cramped conditions in small stone cottages. There were spinning and weaving mills in the village, but most people worked in their own homes.

Less than a year after the family moved to Haworth, Brontë's wife, Maria, died of cancer and four years later he lost his two elder daughters, Maria and Elizabeth. For the remaining children, Charlotte, Branwell, Emily and Anne, the parsonage represented a cherished family home and, for the Brontë girls in particular, its dramatic moorland setting left a lasting, indelible impression on their imagination.

In a letter dated 9 May 1841, Charlotte wrote: 'my home is humble and unattractive to strangers but to me it contains what I shall find nowhere else in the world – the profound and intense affection which brothers and sisters feel for each other when their minds are cast in the same mould.'

One of the first rooms today's visitors see is the dining room. It is appropriate that the tour begins here. This room, which was also a general parlour where family members gathered, is where the sisters fleshed out their novels, endlessly circling the table and reading extracts aloud to each other. All three sisters completed much of their literary output in the dining room: *Jane Eyre*, *Wuthering Heights* and *Agnes Grey* were written here.

It was also in this room, on the horsehair sofa, that Emily died, aged thirty, six days before Christmas. The cause of death was tuberculosis. The second youngest of the Brontë daughters, she refused to accept that she was unwell. It was in this part of the house, too, that Charlotte entertained the writer Elizabeth Gaskell, who became her biographer. By the beginning of the 1850s Charlotte was the sole surviving sister. In solitude she maintained the siblings' tradition of walking round the dining table. The family servant recalled hearing 'Miss Brontë walking, walking on alone.'

Across the hall is Patrick Brontë's study where the dyspeptic curate ate his meals alone and wrote his sermons. From the window he could see the nearby church where he preached on Sundays. Brontë was an honest, decent man who did much to benefit the village community. He established a Sunday School, fought for health improvements and wrote many letters and references on behalf of his parishioners, many of whom were illiterate or ill-educated.

The kitchen is also open to visitors. The furniture and china all belonged to the Brontës and Emily would be found in here, reading and composing poems while she stirred puddings and made bread. On chilly winter evenings the children would gather here to listen to the reminiscences of their faithful servant.

The Brontë sisters took on various household tasks at the parsonage and after their brother Branwell's death, Emily assumed the role of housekeeper, her duties stimulating her imagination, enabling her to write freely and without interruption.

Charlotte converted an old fuel store into a study for her future husband Arthur Bell Nicholls. She added a fireplace, window and door to the hall. On the walls are pew doors from Haworth's former church, which was demolished in 1879. Nicholls acted as Patrick

Brontë's curate and a good deal of parish business was carried out in this room. It is alleged that Charlotte married Nicholls on the rebound after her publisher, George Smith, to whom she was clearly attracted, married the beautiful and highly sociable Elizabeth Blakeway, daughter of a London wine merchant, in 1854. However, once married, Charlotte and Nicholls were extremely happy, although their blissful union was short-lived: she died in childbirth aged thirty-eight. After Charlotte's death, Nicholls continued to live at the parsonage, caring for Brontë senior. Nicholls died in 1906, aged eighty-eight, having outlived his wife by more than half a century.

Charlotte's room, the main bedroom of the house, is where the novelist died with her husband praying at her bedside. Poignantly, personal possessions and items of her clothing, including tiny dresses and shoes, can be seen. Charlotte's mother also died in this room, which is believed to have been Emily's bedroom in the last years of her life.

Adjoining Charlotte's room is the children's study where the Brontë girls studied and played in the time-honoured fashion. It was in this room that the children immersed themselves in their own extraordinary, private world of fantasy and wild imagination. These protracted spells of creativity, involving long hours of reading and writing, would prove to be extremely fruitful in later life.

Completed in 1951 by Jocelyn Horner, a local artist, this bronze statue of Charlotte (seen on the left), Emily and Anne was commissioned by the Brontë Society.

The Brontës' literary genius and the originality of their writing were recognized and applauded during their lifetime. All three women were unworldly, yet they produced acclaimed works of passion and drama. Years after the sisters' untimely deaths, they continue to enthral and inspire generations of readers. The Brontë Parsonage welcomes up to 80,000 visitors annually, including many Japanese fans of the books.

The churchyard, directly in front of the house, is a vivid reminder of the Brontës' time at Haworth. Row upon row of weathered, crumbling gravestones and Gothic memorials, many of them cracked and split by tree growth, march haphazardly towards the boundary wall. It is a perfect evocation of a Victorian churchyard, eerie and dismal and instantly reminiscent of a Brontë novel. The remains of the Brontës lie in the family vault beneath the church, apart from Anne, who is buried at Scarborough, on the North Yorkshire coast, where she died.

Beyond Haworth, amid untamed moorland to the south-west, lie the ruins of Top Withins, said to be the model for Wuthering

The long, lonely hike to Top Withins, now a forlorn ruin, is worth the effort for the fine views and brooding atmosphere. The desolate moorland setting of the house in *Wuthering Heights* matches that of Top Withins.

Heights, the Earnshaw home in Emily Brontë's stirring novel of doomed love and brooding passion. Charlotte describes the house in chapter two in the book:

> Pure, bracing ventilation they must have up there, at all times, indeed: one may guess the power of the north wind, blowing over the edge, by the excessive slant of a few, stunted firs at the end of the house; and by a range of gaunt thorns all stretching their limbs one way, as if craving alms of the sun. Happily, the architect had foresight to build it strong: the narrow windows are deeply set in the wall, and the corners defended with large jutting stones.

Little remains of the farmhouse today, and to get there involves walking several miles along the Pennine Way, one of Britain's most isolated long-distance trails, but the area in which Top Withins is situated conveys a vivid portrait of the setting in *Wuthering Heights*.

The identification of Top Withins as Wuthering Heights was established in the early 1870s when Smith Elder & Co decided to produce an illustrated edition of the Brontë novels. It was generally assumed that the houses described in the books had counterparts in reality. Charlotte's close friend Ellen Nussey was approached with a view to compiling a list of original locations from which the editor could commission illustrations. Nussey suggested Top Withins as the model for Wuthering Heights, though the reason is not clear. Even when complete, Top Withins bore little resemblance to the farmhouse in the book. Clearly, the artist, Wimperis, thought so too. Although he used Top Withins as the basis for the illustration, he enlarged the house and added a further storey. It is quite possible that Emily explored this rugged moorland country on foot and might well have summoned this location to mind when writing *Wuthering Heights*.

Brontë scholars believe that some of the architectural features of the house were drawn from High Sunderland Hall, near Halifax, which has since been demolished. Many visitors to Haworth are compelled to visit the desolate landscape of Emily's imagination and, to a certain extent, the existence of Top Withins fulfils that need.

Charlotte Brontë 1816–55

Charlotte and her two younger sisters were born in Thornton, south-east of York. During the early 1840s Charlotte worked as a teacher and governess in Brussels. She returned to Yorkshire to complete her masterpiece *Jane Eyre* (1847) and two years later she wrote *Shirley*, a novel set during the Luddite riots. By this time her siblings were dead and she lived at the parsonage with her father. When Charlotte died, she left part of an unpublished novel, *Emma*. Two stories by her, *Lily Hart* and *The Secret* were published for the first time in 1978.

Emily Brontë 1818–48

Employed as a governess in Halifax, Emily Brontë's single novel was *Wuthering Heights*, published in 1847 under the name Ellis Bell. The most reclusive of the Brontë sisters, Emily, with Anne, created the Gondal saga, which she continued to write almost to the end of her life.

Anne Brontë 1820–49

Like her two sisters, Anne Brontë worked as a governess but was forced to give up the job because of her brother's infatuation with her employer. *Agnes Grey* (1845), published under the pseudonym Acton Bell, and *The Tenant of Wildfell Hall* (1848), the latter receiving greater acclaim and widely regarded as a feminist classic, were both published towards the end of Anne Brontë's life and although she was a successful novelist, her name and reputation are less well known than those of her two sisters. Twenty of her poems were included in *The Poems of Currer, Ellis and Acton Bell* (1846). She died of tuberculosis.

JAMES HERRIOT'S HOUSE

TELEVISION AND FILM MADE James Herriot a household name and an internationally known author. The daily experiences of a young vet in the years immediately before the Second World War and whose North Yorkshire patch was one of the bleakest and wildest tracts of country in Britain became the subject of a series of hugely popular, semi-autobiographical stories that struck the perfect balance between nostalgia and reality.

The house in Kirkgate in the centre of Thirsk was where Alf Wight lived and worked early in his career as a vet. He used the pen name James Herriot after seeing the Scottish goalkeeper Jim Herriot play for Birmingham City in a televised game against Manchester United.

Herriot's fame sprang from his books; his real name was Alf Wight and he used the pseudonym James Herriot to publish his first volume of memoirs in 1970. By then he was living in Thirsk, a quaint market town on the edge of the spectacular North York Moors. Thirty years earlier Wight moved to the town from Sunderland to join a veterinary practice owned by Donald Sinclair, which the latter had purchased a year earlier.

Donald Sinclair was portrayed in the books as Siegfried Farnon, the mercurial, idiosyncratic senior vet. The practice was run from a house in Kirkgate, just off Thirsk's picturesque cobbled square, and when Wight arrived at the surgery to be interviewed for the post of assistant vet, it became clear that Sinclair, out on calls, had overlooked the appointment. As Wight would soon discover, his endearing absentmindedness was renowned. He waited hours for Sinclair to arrive, settling down in the garden with his back against an acacia tree. Soon, with the warm summer sun beating down on the peaceful garden, Wight was asleep. Eventually, he woke to find his potential employer standing over him, looking unsurprised. It was the start of a long and happy association that would see the two vets eventually working as partners.

Despite the rather primitive conditions and the severity of the Yorkshire climate, it was a way of life in an idyllic corner of England that suited Wight perfectly. He loved the place. 'My Yorkshire, a land of pure air, rocky streams and hidden waterfalls', he wrote.

In 1941, shortly after Wight accepted the offer of becoming assistant to Sinclair, he married Joan Danbury who, at that time, worked as a secretary in a local mill. However, an exotic honeymoon in some far-flung corner of the globe was not for them. Money was tight and it was wartime. Instead, the couple began their married life by tuberculin testing in a nearby village.

The newly-weds both lived and worked at the Kirkgate premises, setting up home on the top floor of the tall Georgian house, in rooms furnished with items from second-hand house sales. As a vet Wight was required to be on duty at all hours of the day and night, often turning out to a remote Dales farm in the depths of winter. Joan kept the books for the business.

One of Wight's abiding memories of life at Kirkgate was, of all things, a fluttering dishcloth. Every morning, as he made his way to the garage at the bottom of the long garden to begin his daily round, he would look back and wave towards the house. Joan would respond by using the dishcloth to wave back. It became a measure of their domestic harmony and one of the more amusing rituals of their long and happy marriage.

After a period of war service, Wight returned to Thirsk. By the time he and Joan moved to another address in the town in 1953, they had two children; James and Rosie. The family was complete. Long after he and the family moved, Wight would continue to look back as he made his way from the practice down the garden path to his car. In his mind's eye he could still see the familiar dishcloth unfurled at the top window of the house.

In the early days, the veterinary practice's clientele came mainly from the local agricultural community and Wight's stories were mostly based on fact, inspired by the dour farming characters of the Yorkshire Dales and his happy memories of attending to their animals.

Wight's son James recalls a magical childhood at Kirkgate where he lived until the age of ten. He remembers playing in the garden and trying to keep warm in the house, which lacked an effective heating system and was often bitterly cold in the winter. As a boy, James wore shorts throughout the year and when he complained to his father of feeling so cold, Wight urged him to run in order to keep warm.

Today, 23 Kirkgate is divided into three distinct visitor areas housed within the same building and known as 'The World of James Herriot'. There is Wight's original marital home and workplace, followed by a television studio with a replica of the same house, as seen in the hugely popular BBC television adaptation of the vet's stories, *All Creatures Great and Small*, which ran for twelve years. The interior of the Thirsk house has been recreated to give an impression of daily life in a vet's practice in the post-war years. Finally, there is a museum of veterinary science, the only centre of its kind in the

The Fold Yard on display at Kirkgate is a typical example of an enclosure for sheep or cattle. Alf Wight would have seen a great many on his rounds through the Yorkshire Dales.

country devoted to the subject. The entire complex is acknowledged as an established visitor attraction which has done much to boost the Yorkshire tourist economy.

My first visit to Yorkshire, a family holiday in the mid-1970s, coincided with my introduction to the Herriot stories. What struck me most about these charming tales was Alf Wight's uncomplicated writing style and commonplace, often light-hearted narrative. His gift as a writer lay not in eloquent purple prose but in his ability to use the simplest passages to convey what he saw around him. Wight's vivid description of the Yorkshire Dales brought the region instantly to life, but his stories were not simply about saving and rescuing animals. Wight's experiences as a vet brought him into contact with a host of colourful characters and rural traditions, reflecting a way of life that, alas, has gone forever. The books, while continuing to capture the imagination of millions of readers, represent a fascinating social document of the time.

James Herriot (Alf Wight) 1916–95

Born in Sunderland, Alf Wight was raised in Glasgow where he qualified as a veterinary surgeon at the city's Veterinary College. He moved to Thirsk soon after the outbreak of the Second World War, where he remained for the rest of his life, with the exception of his wartime service in the RAF.

His first book *If Only They Could Talk*, was written in 1966, by which time Wight was fifty years of age, and published in 1970. Seven further volumes chronicling his life as a vet followed and sales of all James Herriot titles are now in excess of 80 million. Wight died of cancer at his home near Thirsk at the age of seventy-eight.

SHANDY HALL

AT FIRST GLANCE, THE period roadside house on the western edge of the village of Coxwold appears like countless other picturesque, solidly constructed dwellings in this corner of North Yorkshire, but look closely at the name and the inscription above the door and you get a very different impression. Shandy Hall is far from grand but its place in English literature is deeply rooted. This is a house with impeccable literary credentials.

Shandy Hall, a building of great antiquity, thought to have been built around 1430, first appeared on the map as the local parsonage. Originally a timber-framed open-hall house, it was substantially remodelled in the seventeenth century. Shandy Hall's most famous resident, Laurence Sterne, was appointed curate of Coxwold's parish church of St Michael's and settled here with his wife, Elizabeth, and daughter, Lydia, in 1760.

The house changed in appearance again during Sterne's tenure. Referring to it as his 'sweet retreat', he added a Georgian extension, which remains one of Shandy Hall's most distinctive features. The garden includes Sterne's summerhouse or 'sweet pavilion'.

The year 1760 proved to be a crucial turning point in the life and fortunes of Laurence Sterne. The previous year saw the publication of the first two volumes of his first novel, *The Life and Opinions of Tristram Shandy*, which Sterne published at his own expense, borrowing the money to pay for its initial print run. By now middle-aged and anxious about the success of the book, Sterne, a noted

Laurence Sterne left his mark on Shandy Hall; he created a new garden front and made various improvements to the interior of 'my Shandy castle.' The house lies close to the road, on the edge of Coxwold.

philanderer, began a brief affair with a singer, Kitty Fourmantel.

To Sterne's relief, his fears for *Tristram Shandy* proved to be misjudged. The book was an outstanding success. There were several further editions and he also published two volumes of his sermons. Sterne was the toast of the literary world and fêted wherever he went. He even became the subject of a portrait by Sir Joshua Reynolds, which raised his profile and changed people's perception of him long before the era of modern media. Although he came to writing late in life, Sterne's destiny was assured. He was now a man of considerable stature.

Around this time, Sterne was offered the living at Coxwold and the family rented the old parsonage, which he and his friends dubbed 'Shandy Hall' after the fictional home of the Shandy family in the novel. The word 'shandy' has its origins locally and means odd or crackbrained.

Sterne's modest income from the church was boosted significantly by increased book sales, giving him a welcome sense of security at last. Adding to the picture of contentment was Shandy Hall's glorious setting at the southern foot of the Hambleton Hills. Sterne was happiest at Coxwold where in 1761, he recorded 'good air, a quiet retreat, and quiet reflections along with it … together do wonders'. Life was good.

His remaining years were spent writing. Although Sterne regularly journeyed to London, and even overseas to France and Italy, he always returned to Shandy Hall, his 'philosophical hut', to write: 'I shall write as long as I live, 'tis in fact my hobby horse. … My daughter Lydia helps to copy for me – and my wife knits and listens as I read my chapters.'

Little has changed at Shandy Hall since Laurence Sterne lived there. The rooms reveal first editions of the author's work, manuscripts, well-stocked bookshelves, paintings and other ephemera. With the curator's help and a little imagination, it is possible to picture Sterne in his study at Shandy Hall. Impulsive and untidy, he would often work long into the night, his mind teeming with ideas and ink spilling across his desk as he rushed to commit the words to paper. His mode of dress was often unorthodox to say the least. 'Here I am sitting,' he wrote during one very hot summer, 'in a purple jerkin and yellow pair of slippers, without either wig or cap on.'

Ensconced in his small study at Shandy Hall, Sterne's output during the last years of his life was astonishing. Most prominent and demanding of his time were the remaining seven volumes of *Tristram Shandy*. Notable in Sterne's gallery of characters is the eccentric, richly drawn Uncle Toby, one of the finest creations in English literature. At the heart of the books is the Shandy family: Walter Shandy, his wife Elizabeth and their son Tristram.

It is Tristram who acts as narrator, relating the story of his life and that of his family, although Sterne cleverly weaves Tristram's narrative into a rambling diatribe characterized by verbosity and digression. However, the novels are benign; Sterne exhibits no malice. Instead, they show the author to be wonderfully flippant, comic, poetic and deeply philosophical. Playing around with the theme of identity and peppered with visual jokes, riddles and surprises, the whimsical writing confirms Sterne's genius.

Shandy Hall, as it is described in the first two volumes, is purely the work of the author's imagination. Thereafter, Sterne was writing with his parsonage home in mind. As curator Patrick Wildgust has said on many occasions: 'Clearly, Shandy Hall did inform his work. In terms of place, visitors are about as close to the art of writing the book as it is possible to be.'

Abandoned by his wife, Sterne's final stage of life was poignant. Only months before his death, while visiting a friend in London, he met and fell deeply in love with Eliza Draper, a young married woman of twenty-three who had ambitions to be a writer. The age gap between them – thirty years – was significant, but Sterne was undeterred. However, the love affair did not end happily. Eliza eventually sailed for India, where her husband was an official based in Bombay.

Overwhelmed by loneliness and despair, Sterne returned to Coxwold and prepared a room at Shandy Hall, in the vain hope that Eliza would one day visit him there: 'a neat little simple elegant room, overlooked only by the sun,' he wrote. 'I sit here ... as solitary as a tom cat, which by the bye is all the company I keep – he follows me from the parlour, to the kitchen, into the garden, and every place.'

The stone tablet over the front entrance to Shandy Hall recalls that Laurence Sterne dwelt here 'many years incumbent of Coxwold.' In the 1960s, the house looked very different – blighted by dry rot and death-watch beetle.

In its time Shandy Hall has also been a farmhouse and the residence of a surgeon. By the mid-1960s it was in a poor state of repair and there were many who believed it should be consigned to history. 'Madness to try and restore such a structure; another winter and it will collapse', was the general consensus. However, a trust was established in 1967, almost two hundred years after Sterne's death, to rescue the house from ruin and oblivion.

Laurence Sterne 1713–68

The son of an infantry ensign, Sterne was born in Clonmel, County Tipperary. He was educated at Halifax Grammar School in West Yorkshire and at Jesus College, Cambridge. Sterne was ordained in 1738 and was subsequently appointed to the living of Sutton-on-the-Forest, between Coxwold and York. In later life, as his health began to fail, he wrote *A Sentimental Journey through France and Italy*, a work of fiction largely inspired by his travels in Europe. The novel was published shortly before his death.

HILL TOP

THE WRITER AND ILLUSTRATOR Beatrix Potter moved to Hill Top, a seventeenth-century farmhouse near Lake Windermere, in 1905, following the sudden death of her fiancé and publisher, Norman Warne, as the result of leukaemia. Potter had become acquainted with the region through long family holidays in the Lakes, especially the area between Coniston and Windermere, which she described as 'very pretty hilly country, but not wild like Keswick or Ullswater'. The earnings from her books, combined with a small legacy from an aunt, enabled her to buy Hill Top Farm in the village of Near Sawrey. As Lakeland farmhouses went, it was unremarkable, with rough-cast walls and a slate roof.

Though Hill Top might have appeared simple and unpretentious to the casual observer, Potter was entirely comfortable with her decision to buy the farm. She was not a countrywoman – she lived in London with her parents until 1913 – but the setting was picturesque and the place had much charm and character, which appealed to her. She loved Hill Top's topsy-turvy quirkiness – the herbs and flowers lining the path, the rambling pink rose that spread itself across the front of the house and the beehives hidden in a niche in the stone wall behind the rhubarb patch.

Not surprisingly, Hill Top and its surroundings fuelled her imagination and she painstakingly reproduced much of what she saw and cherished in her delightful book illustrations. Tom Kitten, Samuel Whiskers and Jemima Puddleduck were all created here and the outstanding success of the recent film about Potter's life has introduced her work to a new audience.

The garden appears in *The Tale of Tom Kitten* (1907) and the seventeenth- and eighteenth-century furniture, acquired at local sales, features in many of the later stories – among them a wonderful dresser, which can be identified in *The Tailor of Gloucester* (1903) and *The Tale of Samuel Whiskers* (1908). The nearby seventeenth-century Tower Bank Arms features in *The Tale of Jemima Puddle-Duck* (1908) – even the name of the pub is seen in the illustration – and *The Tale of Ginger and Pickles* (1909) includes the former village shop at Sawrey.

At the rear of the farmhouse is the New Room, once filled with manuscripts and paintings. The constant throng of visitors eventually made it impractical to keep them here. In this room Potter produced seven of her best-loved and most successful books, using the oak bureau as her writing desk.

Beatrix Potter did not live permanently at Hill Top. She carried out various alterations and improvements to the house, adding a wing for the tenant farmer John Cannon who was her farm manager and foreman. Cannon's expert knowledge and experience allowed him to play a key role in maintaining Hill Top as a successful farming enterprise.

Potter was careful to retain Hill Top's character and many of its original features, including the fireplace, which she reproduced in several books. The smallest details and commonplace, everyday features never escaped her notice.

To visit Hill Top is to enter Potter's extraordinary world of books and watercolours. Many of the subjects she chose to paint or sketch over the years have been so authentically recreated that they are instantly recognizable in reality, such is the level of accuracy. Many of these illustrations were invaluable when the National Trust began re-creating the farmhouse's garden and interior to reflect Potter's time at Hill Top.

Beatrix Potter eventually married in 1913 at the age of forty-seven. Her husband was William Heelis, a local solicitor who acted for her. By this time she had established an impressive property portfolio, including Castle Farm, her marital home, in Sawrey. Her literary success allowed her to buy land as well; she acquired a total of 4,000 acres. She also bred sheep – Herdwicks in particular, a rare breed found only in the Lake District.

The years following the First World War represented a settled period in Potter's life. Happily married, she continued to write and, though childless, she was close to her husband's extended family. By the late 1930s, however, the future in this tranquil corner of the country looked uncertain once more. The prospect of yet another World War was a grim one, but for Beatrix Potter there were other deeper issues to address. By now, her own story was drawing to a close. Potter's powers were failing and it became clear she would need to undergo an operation. 'Most times it has been an effort to walk to Hill Top,' she wrote. 'I am so glad I was feeling particularly well last week, and I have seen the snowdrops again ... the whole world seems to be rushing to Armageddon. But not even Hitler can damage the fells.'

However, despite her frailty, Potter hadn't lost her spirit. She rallied, living through four more productive and rewarding years. 'I am incredibly well,' she wrote to her cousin in 1939, 'and can do a bit of weeding when it is not too hot.' It was typical of Potter to roll up her sleeves and apply herself diligently to physical tasks.

She bequeathed Hill Top to the National Trust, stipulating that it be left exactly as it was when she lived there. She wanted the house to reflect her many happy years there and her stamp on the place. Littered with treasured furniture, personal mementoes and casually placed possessions, Hill Top's interior has been arranged to convey to visitors the impression that Potter has simply gone out for a stroll. During her years in the Lake District she developed a passion for land conservation and became one of the National Trust's most prominent early benefactors, bequeathing her land and a total of fifteen farms to the charity.

Generations of children have been drawn to Potter's magical world over the years. Many have visited Hill Top to experience and savour the setting and to see where she produced what are now acknowledged as enduring classics of literature, written with great honesty and without a trace of sentimentality. Beatrix Potter has entertained children and adults alike for more than a century, but more importantly the stories express her deep love and affection for the hills and valleys of her cherished Lake District.

Beatrix Potter 1866–1943

Beatrix Potter was born in Kensington, London. Her father was a lawyer who inherited a large fortune in 1883. Delicate and frail, Potter was taught by governesses and looked after by nurses. As children, she and her brother became fascinated by the natural world around them, observing and recording the daily habits of animals and birds and, from an early age, the two siblings cared for various pets. Potter, who once lived at Camfield Place, near Hatfield in Hertfordshire, later the home of the romantic novelist Barbara Cartland, taught herself to draw and paint at an early age. By the end of her life she had produced twenty-two books. Today, she is acknowledged as the greatest and most gifted writer and illustrator of picture-story books of her generation, known and respected throughout the world for her sharp, incisive prose, impressively strong storylines and beautifully observed pictures.

WORDSWORTH HOUSE

ONE OF THE LOVELIEST and most interesting features of Grade I-listed Wordsworth House is the River Derwent, which runs behind the house where the poet was born and raised in the latter years of the eighteenth century. The river was one of the delights of living in this grand Georgian town house in the centre of Cockermouth, along with the garden, and it was where the poet sought his earliest inspiration.

> *When, having left his mountains, to the towers*
> *Of Cockermouth that beauteous river came,*
> *Behind my father's house he passed, close by,*
> *Along the margin of our terrace walk.*

The opening lines of *The Prelude* (1805–6) convey his love of the river here. The Derwent, which scurries through Cockermouth on its way to the sea at Workington eight miles away, was 'the playmate whom we dearly lov'd'. Wordsworth regarded it as 'the fairest of all rivers'.

The Wordsworth family didn't own the house. William's father was land agent to Sir James Lowther, a landowner and influential figure in the area, whose father built Whitehaven and its port along the coast. The Wordsworths were his tenants.

William Wordsworth's love of and preoccupation with literature evolved in his father's library in the house. It was here that he studied the works of Shakespeare and Milton, among others. The garden was where he and his younger sister, Dorothy, developed their appreciation of nature. Many of the original features remain and can be identified: the terrace where the two children played, the grassy banks lining the Derwent and the meadow on the far side of it.

Inside, the house is filled with Georgian furniture, predominantly Hepplewhite and Chippendale. The parlour and dining room have displays of Staffordshire and Coalport china. On the first floor in the drawing room are several rococo console tables and an impressive collection of prints, drawings and paintings of Lake District scenes.

Wordsworth's time at Cockermouth was short. His mother died when he was eight and his father five years later. The Wordsworth children were subsequently cared for by relatives. The house remained in private hands until the 1930s when Cockermouth Library tried unsuccessfully to acquire it. Instead, a local bus company bought the house with the intention of demolishing it to make way for a bus station. The plan failed, thanks to a strongly fought campaign, supported by the people of Cockermouth, and in 1938 Wordsworth House was given to the National Trust. In June the following year it opened its doors to the public.

Over the years Wordsworth's childhood home has been the subject of discussion, debate and general interest – Pevsner described it as 'quite a swagger house for such a town' in his book *The Buildings of England – Cumberland and Westmorland* – and in 2009 Wordsworth House made headlines when floodwater threatened to destroy the contents six years after the National Trust undertook a major revamp of the property. The objective had been to interpret a mid-eighteenth century family home as accurately as possible. Thankfully, volunteers were able to rescue valuable artefacts by moving them to the upper floors.

DOVE COTTAGE

IT WAS JUST FIVE days before Christmas when William Wordsworth and his sister Dorothy moved into Dove Cottage. The year was 1799 and the home they had acquired was a modest early seventeenth-century dwelling adorned with dazzling roses and jasmine. Surrounded by the natural beauty of the Lake District and built of stone walls with a roof of local slate, the cottage conformed perfectly to the idea of a simple, unpretentious country retreat. Until six years previously, it had been a pub, the Dove and Olive Branch.

Before moving to Dove Cottage, for which they paid an annual rent of £5, William and Dorothy spent much of their time apart. However, as they approached thirty, they craved a quiet, comfortable routine where they could indulge in 'plain living but high thinking'.

Wordsworth spent the most productive years of his life at Dove Cottage. Tucked into a hillside, the ground-floor rooms were dark and gloomy. Candles made from lamb fat were used to improve the lighting.

Much brighter than the ground floor, the upstairs sitting room was the obvious choice for reading and writing.

It was in the upstairs sitting room at Dove Cottage that Wordsworth wrote some of his greatest and best-loved poems, including 'Resolution and Independence' and 'Daffodils'. His sister wrote that he 'laboured in that one room, common to all the family, to all visitors.' As a poet, his time at Dove Cottage represented his most productive period and while he wrote, Dorothy looked after the house, tended the garden and updated her journal, which she kept between 1800 and 1803.

The diary proved to be an invaluable document, in which she gave a detailed account of everyday life at Dove Cottage. It also provided inspiration for William, who recalled the pleasure of living in this rural seclusion and the obvious delight he took in Dorothy's company in his poem 'Home at Grasmere'.

The blissful, harmonious atmosphere that pervaded Dove Cottage prevailed for several years until suddenly daily life in the household took a very different direction when William married Mary Hutchinson and brought his bride to live with them at Grasmere. The comfortable routine at Dove Cottage became even less familiar with the arrival of their three children, John, Dora and Thomas, all born within four years in the downstairs bedroom.

Not surprisingly, the children had a disruptive influence on life at Dove Cottage but there were other forms of chaos. Samuel Taylor Coleridge, with whom Wordsworth first saw Dove Cottage while

The kitchen parlour at Dove Cottage, known by William and Dorothy Wordsworth as the 'houseplace'. This was possibly the busiest room in the house and it was here that meals were taken and various chores completed.

on a walking tour of the Lakes, was a frequent visitor who would arrive unexpectedly at all hours of the day and night, on occasions bringing children, and Sir Walter Scott, another guest, grew so tired of the bowlfuls of porridge he was fed that he hauled himself out of his bedroom window to seek an alternative, more appealing diet at the village inn.

After William's marriage to Mary, Sara, her unmarried sister, also took up residence at the cottage. (Sara caught Coleridge's eye during one of his many visits and he fell in love with her. The poet, who was unhappily married, chose to leave his wife for Sara.) 'We are crammed in our little nest edge-full,' wrote Dorothy in 1806. It must have been a far cry from the early days at Dove Cottage when she and her brother were the sole occupants and life would have been largely quiet and uneventful by comparison.

In 1808, nearly ten years after Wordsworth and his sister moved to Grasmere, it was increasingly apparent that Dove Cottage had outgrown its usefulness and the family moved to larger premises in the village. Dove Cottage was leased to the poet Thomas De Quincy who had also been one of the regular guests at Dove Cottage.

Dove Cottage was acquired by the Wordsworth Trust in 1890 and opened to visitors the following year. Wordsworth described Grasmere as 'the loveliest spot that man hath ever found'.

RYDAL MOUNT

IN THE YEARS FOLLOWING Wordsworth's tenure of Dove Cottage, he and his wife Mary experienced personal tragedy. They lost two of their children in 1812 while living at the Old Rectory in Grasmere, their second place of residence since leaving Dove Cottage. The Old Rectory's close proximity to the church, where the infants were buried, was a constant reminder of the family's painful loss and a decision was taken by the couple to move further away. Their next home was Rydal Mount in Ambleside and it was here Wordsworth lived for the rest of his life.

William and Mary, accompanied by their three surviving children, his sister Dorothy and Mary's sibling, Sara, took up residence in 1813. Prior to the move the poet found himself in financial difficulties and there had been a great deal of animosity between him and his old friend Samuel Taylor Coleridge following a bitter quarrel fuelled by personal and professional jealousy. The move to Rydal Mount eased the tension.

The same year saw an improvement in Wordsworth's income following his appointment as Distributor of Stamps in the county of Westmorland. Increased funds enabled the poet and his family to live more comfortably, and Dorothy also raised her brother's spirits by telling him that in her opinion Rydal Mount was 'the nicest place in the world for children'. And so it was to the casual observer.

However, in reality the rather grandly named Rydal Mount began life as a modest sixteenth-century farm labourer's cottage and over the years was enlarged and embellished to become a reasonably sized family villa. With its steeply sloping four-acre garden and charming setting on the banks of Rydal Water, the house suited its master admirably: Wordsworth, a respected poet, public servant and country gentleman one day surely in line for the greatest prize of all – Poet Laureate.

That didn't happen until 1843, by which time Wordsworth's life was drawing to a close. However, in the years leading up to the appointment he wrote a great many poems and entertained many eminent visitors at Rydal Mount, including Swinburne, who was only a child at the time, Matthew Arnold and Nathaniel Hawthorne.

Wordsworth's habit of composing verse outdoors and then memorizing it before returning home was highlighted by his servant at Rydal Mount, who pointed out that the library was 'where he keeps his books: his study is out of doors'. This somewhat romanticized statement is not strictly correct as Wordsworth did have his own study at the top of the house. It may have been where the great poet laboured for hours and days but the view from his study – a majestic landscape of fells and lakes – was a reminder of the natural beauty of the great outdoors, where he found true inspiration.

The principal bedroom at Rydal Mount overlooked nearby Dora's Field, which Wordsworth bought when he believed his tenancy of the house would not be extended. His intention was to build a house on the land. However, his fears proved unfounded as the lease continued to be renewed. He presented the plot to his daughter, Dora, though sadly she died of tuberculosis three years before her father. Today, in spring, appropriately, the field is covered with a bright yellow carpet of daffodils.

William Wordsworth 1770–1850

Radical as a youth and orphaned at an early age, Wordsworth was one of nature's most ardent enthusiasts. He was educated at Hawkshead in the Lake District before attending Cambridge University (1787–91). He embarked on a walking tour of France and Switzerland and later began an affair with Annette Vallon, who bore him a daughter. While in France, Wordsworth became a devoted republican. He, his sister, Dorothy, and their friend Samuel Taylor Coleridge eventually settled in Somerset where, with Coleridge, he composed the *Lyrical Ballads* (1798), which included Wordsworth's 'Tintern Abbey'. His later work, including his ode 'Intimations of Immortality' (1807), written after he and Dorothy moved to Grasmere, cemented his reputation as the greatest poet of his age. His poetic autobiography *The Prelude* was published posthumously in 1850.

Dorothy Wordsworth 1771–1855

Like her brother, Dorothy was orphaned at an early age: her father died when she was twelve and she went to live with her aunt, Elizabeth Threlkeld, in West Yorkshire. William's only sister, Dorothy was his constant companion, accompanying him on tours of the Isle of Man, Scotland and Europe. Her love of, and devotion to, her natural surroundings is well chronicled, although her writing was mainly in the form of letters, poems, diary entries and various short stories. In 1829, aged fifty-eight, she suffered a breakdown from which she never fully recovered. She never married.

SCOTLAND

ANGUS

THE HOUSE OF DUN

THE SCOTTISH POET AND novelist Violet Jacob, born Violet Augusta Mary Frederica Kennedy-Erskine, came from an ancient, aristocratic family who had owned the Dun estate for centuries. Four miles west of Montrose, on Scotland's remote north-east coast, the House of Dun was built in 1730 for David Erskine, the thirteenth Laird of Dun and a distinguished judge of the Scottish Court of Session, who, beneath this cloak of respectability, was a covert Jacobite. Violet's grandmother, Augusta, was an illegitimate daughter of the Duke of Clarence (later William IV) and the actress Dorothy Jordan. These fascinating aspects of Jacob's past, highlighting colourful examples of scandal and intrigue in her family, almost certainly helped to stimulate her imagination as a writer.

Before the Scottish Renaissance of the 1920s, Scots was associated with the lower classes and, as such, was considered to be vulgar and inferior to English. All the more extraordinary, then, that the young aristocrat Jacob developed an ear for Scottish vernacular. Indeed, as a child she seems to have mixed freely with locals and acquired a lively command of Scots, prompting one person to comment later 'as a bairn she was aye in and oot amo' the plooman's feet at the Mains O' Dun'. Educated at home, Jacob was happy and content growing up in the picturesque countryside of Angus, formerly Forfarshire, and listening to the broad Scots dialect of the region. Jacob wrote many short stories about the people, landscape and language of this lovely corner of Scotland and, in 1931, she published her family history, *The Lairds of Dun*.

Violet Jacob's first book, a light-hearted narrative poem in Scots, written with William Douglas Campbell and which she also illustrated, was published in 1888. She wrote sparingly, but her later work is much stronger and more effective, particularly her contribution to fiction. Perhaps the finest example of this is *Flemington*, published in 1911, a powerful novel set mainly in Scotland after the Jacobite uprising and defeat at Culloden and which reflects the political turmoil of the period. The writer John Buchan considered *Flemington* to be '... the best Scots romance since *The Master of Ballantrae*.' Full of action and intrigue, the story was influenced and shaped by Jacob's own family history. The narrative is taut and the Angus sequences are vividly drawn and evocative. The main character, David Logie of Banillo, is clearly modelled on her ancestor David Erskine, and the estate she describes is almost certainly based on the House of Dun.

Another popular work of fiction is *The Interloper* (1904) and here, too, Jacob draws heavily on her native Angus. Set in the early nineteenth century, the plot concerns a young man who returns from Spain to inherit his Scottish estate. The story is strong and entertaining, but what sets it apart from other historical romances of the period is the remarkable use of authentic Scots dialogue in the writing.

Seventeen years prior to the publication of *Flemington*, its author had married Arthur Otway Jacob, an Irishman who served as a lieutenant with the 20th Royal Hussars, a cavalry regiment of the British army. Following the transfer of his regiment, Violet Jacob joined her husband in India. Circumstances dictated that her life would now be spent far from her roots in Angus, though she eventually returned to the country of her birth in 1936, following her husband's death. During her final years she moved to Marywell House near Kirriemuir, close to the birthplace of J. M. Barrie.

The House of Dun is managed by the National Trust for Scotland and has been open to members of the public since 1989. Inside, the house is crammed with period furniture and *objets d'art*. One of the most striking features is the ornate relief plasterwork, which is decorated in exuberant fashion with Jacobite symbolism. The buildings in the courtyard consist of a hen house, a potting shed and a gamekeeper's workshop. The House of Dun stands amid splendid Victorian gardens and woodlands.

Violet Jacob 1863–1946

Violet Jacob, née Kennedy-Erskine, was born at the House of Dun in the county of Angus. She was the eldest of the three surviving children of William Henry Kennedy-Erskine, Laird of Dun, and his wife Catherine. One of her ancestors was John Erskine, fifth Laird of Dun, who was a moderator of the general assembly of the Church of Scotland and a friend of the religious reformer John Knox. The years Violet Jacob and her husband spent in India represented one of the happiest periods of her life and while there she recorded her experiences and observations in various diaries and letters, which were later published. She also painted many rare flowers.

Jacob lost her only child, Harry, who died, aged twenty, of wounds sustained at the Battle of the Somme. The subsequent years left her unsettled and distraught as she continued to grieve for him. During this period, she concentrated on poetry and prose and many of her poems were initially published in *Country Life*. Her first collection was *Songs of Angus* (1915). *The Scottish Poems of Violet Jacob* (1944) includes some of her best work. Described as charming and handsome, Violet Jacob is acknowledged as a major influence among the young poets who dedicated themselves to the regeneration of Scots as a literary language. Her fiction can be interpreted as a history of Scotland. She died of heart disease just six days short of her eighty-third birthday.

J.M. BARRIE'S BIRTHPLACE

JAMES MATTHEW (J.M.) BARRIE'S fantasy world of magic and make-believe is a legacy of childhood – a rosy, nostalgic picture of youthful innocence and eternal adventure that we carry with us in our mind's eye through the different stages of life.

Barrie's enduring masterpiece, *Peter Pan*, has entertained count-less generations over the years and continues to find new audiences today, captivating both children and adults with its many varied interpretations – as a play, a book, a film and even a pantomime. In a sense, we cannot escape its spell, but then nor do we want to.

Barrie's literary inspiration can be traced to a quiet corner of Angus, not far from the north-east coast of Scotland. The small town of Kirriemuir, where the writer was born, became the village of Thrums in *Auld Licht Idyllis, A Window in Thrums* (1890) and *The Little Minister* (1891). Thrums is a technical term in the weaving industry meaning 'the ends of the threads'. Close by is Kirriemuir Hill, where Barrie played as a child and was inspired to create Peter Pan, the boy who never grew up.

Number 9 Brechin Road is the famed writer's birthplace, a modest whitewashed cottage reflecting Barrie's humble, working-class origins. His father was a handloom weaver and young James was the ninth of ten children. The Calvinist family lived a humdrum, uneventful existence in this tight-knit community in the foothills of the Grampians.

However, the predictable pattern of daily life was suddenly and brutally shattered when Barrie was only six: his older brother David died in an ice-skating accident just before his fourteenth birthday. Their mother was distraught, finding comfort in the belief that her favourite child would not grow old. David became the boy who never grew up; he was immortal.

The young James attempted to comfort his mother by emulating his brother, taking to wearing his clothes, whistling merrily in the style of the older boy and generally behaving like him. In his biography of his mother, *Margaret Ogilvy*, Barrie describes the poignant spectacle of David's coffin being laid on the kitchen table.

The memory of Barrie's early childhood at Brechin Road would remain with him in his later years, this crucial formative period in the writer's life leaving an indelible impression on his imagination. According to his dedication in the front of the book of *Peter Pan*, it was the communal wash-house that provided the model for 'the little house the Lost Boys built in the Never Land for Wendy'.

J.M. Barrie left Kirriemuir when he was eight to be educated in Glasgow where one of his older siblings taught. Returning to the family home in Brechin Road, after graduating from university, Barrie wrote an article based on his mother's memories of, and stories about, Kirriemuir. He submitted the piece to a London newspaper – the *St James's Gazette* – and the editor agreed to publish it, commissioning further copy on the same theme, which then became the basis for his books about Thrums.

He returned to Kirriemuir on occasion and during one

memorable visit in 1930 he received the freedom of the borough. A crowd of ten thousand welcomed him back to his hometown.

On his death, Barrie's obituary in *The Times* said: 'He had discovered that literature could be made out of his own people, the people of Kirriemuir. He called the place Thrums and made it famous.'

J.M. Barrie 1860–1937

After settling in London in the 1880s, Barrie became a regular contributor to the *St James's Gazette* and *British Weekly*, writing under the name of Gavin Ogilvy. His critically acclaimed social satire *The Admirable Crichton* was published in 1902 and the same year saw the debut of his greatest creation, Peter Pan, in the novel *The Little White Bird*. Two years later Barrie cemented his reputation by reviving the character, this time making him the eponymous hero of the story. Barrie wrote *Peter Pan* first as a stage play and then later adapted it as a novel. It was while living in London that he befriended the children of the Llewellyn-Davies family whom he often encountered while out walking in Kensington Gardens; he was appointed their guardian following the deaths of their parents and it was they who provided the inspiration for the Lost Boys and Wendy Darling's brothers in *Peter Pan*. Later plays include *Dear Brutus* (1917) and *Mary Rose* (1920).

Great Ormond Street Hospital for Sick Children is strongly associated with Barrie, who bequeathed the royalties from *Peter Pan* to the hospital. He became a baronet in 1922 and Chancellor of Edinburgh University in 1930. Barrie married an actress, Mary Ansell, in 1894; they divorced in 1909.

AYRSHIRE

BURNS COTTAGE

ROBERT BURNS, THE MAN who gave Scotland and the whole world one of the most enduring and evocative songs of farewell ever written, was born in 1759 at Alloway in South Ayrshire. Although the words of 'Auld Lang Syne' are largely obscure and incomprehensible to most people, there are many Burns devotees – especially in his native land – who recall, albeit briefly as the old year vanishes into an alcohol-induced haze, the memory of the man who penned those famous lyrics in 1788. The poem was set to the tune of a traditional folk song. It is because of this and many other poems that Burns would become Scotland's favourite son and national Bard.

Today, the cottage where Burns was born, the eldest of seven children, is acknowledged as Scotland's greatest literary shrine, yet the building is far from grand. The tiny whitewashed dwelling, constructed of thatch and clay, was built by Burns's father, William, in 1757, two years before the arrival of his famous offspring on 25 January, a date that would in time become the subject of traditional Scottish festivities, including feasting and drinking, and which is still marked today all over the world by Burns Night.

At the time of his birth, the family name was actually Burnes. His Calvinist father was a poor farmer and failed market gardener from Kincardineshire; his mother a local girl. The cottage – the 'auld cley biggin' – consisted of one main room in which the family cooked, ate, read, spun, made cheese and slept. The children used a makeshift pull-out cot and, later, a platform erected above their parents' bed. The animals sheltered in an adjacent part of the cottage, the heat from their presence no doubt helping to warm the building. It was a primitive and rudimentary existence, even by the standards of the time.

Despite the harshness of life in the Ayrshire countryside, young Robert learnt to read and write and even attended a local school. His father read the Bible to his children and ensured they received a proper education. He also put aside enough money to hire a school-teacher, John Murdoch, to tutor the boy and later dispatched Robert to stay with the man at the nearby grammar school.

When Burns was eight the family moved to Mount Oliphant, a farm near Ayr, where William Burnes became a tenant farmer. As a boy, Robert helped his father as much as his school commitments would allow, working with him on the land and assisting him with the gathering in of the harvest. By now his early life at the Alloway cottage of his birth would be a memory, but those vital impressions of his time there would have been imprinted in his imagination. Many local landmarks feature in his poems, written in local dialect in celebration of a pre-industrial Scotland.

The simple dwelling of Burns's early childhood has experienced a varied history since he lived there. A landlord spotted the potential for cashing in on Burns's fame and reputation and turned the poet's birthplace into a pub. More than a hundred and fifty years after Robert Burns was born inside the cottage, it became a somewhat unlikely target for violence when several members of the Suffragette movement tried to set light to it in 1914.

Almost one hundred years earlier, in more tranquil times, the cottage was visited by John Keats, who wrote: 'I had no Conception that the native place of Burns was so beautiful – the Idea I had was more desolate.... Besides all the Beauty, there were the Mountains of Arran Isle, black and huge over the Sea.'

In a 2009 poll, television viewers voted Robert Burns the 'Greatest Ever Scot' and his song 'Is There for Honest Poverty' opened the new Scottish Parliament in 1999. The cottage at Alloway is one of Scotland's most popular tourist destinations, with a new museum – the Robert Burns Birthplace Museum – allowing the poet's collection of precious manuscripts, correspondence and artefacts to be housed in one building.

Robert Burns 1759–96

After his father's death in 1784, Robert Burns continued to farm, although his efforts to work the land were never wholly successful. Two years later a collection of his poetry was published to immediate critical acclaim and, by the time his one narrative poem *Tam O'Shanter* was published in 1791, he had written numerous lines of verse and a great many songs, including 'A Red, Red Rose', 'The Banks o'Doon', and 'Ye Jacobites by Name'. He married Jean Armour in 1788. Despite this, throughout his adult life he conducted numerous affairs with other women, his good looks and physical appeal proving to be a distinct advantage.

He died of rheumatic heart disease at the young age of thirty-seven.

THE BORDERS

ABBOTSFORD

TOURISTS GENERALLY CONCEDE THAT the Scottish Borders region is defined by some of the wildest and most spectacular scenery in Britain. The novelist and poet Sir Walter Scott was so moved by its remoteness and grandeur that he wrote:

> To my eye, these grey hills and all this wild border country have beauties peculiar to themselves. I like the very nakedness of the land; it has something bold and stern and solitary about it. If I did not see the heather at least once a year I think I should die.

Scott devoted much of his time to the preservation of what little remained of the region's beautiful but battle-scarred abbeys, thus keeping alive the spirit and character of the Borders. He had known this rugged landscape since boyhood and his abiding love of it is evident in his writing. From the moment he first set eyes

The very remoteness and beauty of the surrounding Borders prompted Sir Walter Scott to settle here and rebuild the original farm house in a style befitting his newly earned status as a popular writer.

on the Border country, Scott was captivated by its long history of lawlessness, battle and bloodshed, its tradition of ballads and folklore, and its wonderful sense of peace and tranquillity. It was this rich legacy that inspired much of his work. The Scotland of Scott's imagination continues to enthral readers today.

When Scott acquired Abbotsford in 1812 it was a very different place from what it became. Known as the Clarty Hole (dirty hollow), it was little more than a marshy farm house with a barn adjacent to a filthy pond. Scott's original vision for the site was a cottage retreat. He wrote:

> My present intention is to have only two spare bedrooms with dressing rooms, each of which will have, on a pinch, a couch bed, but I cannot relinquish my Border principle of accommodating all the cousins and duniwastles who will rather sleep on chairs and on the floor and in the hayloft, than be absent when folks are gathered together.

Scott's cottage project was abandoned in 1814 following the death of his architect. However, the writer would not be beaten. He was determined to build a home of his own choosing. Two years later his thoughts were occupied by the prospect of a new house, commissioning plans from William Atkinson, a London architect. Work began in 1817 and lasted for two years. The final result should have been enough, but when Scott was awarded a baronetcy in 1818 he felt compelled to own a house that was commensurate with his elevated status. Once again building work began, but this time the design was on a much grander scale.

In 1820, Scott wrote to his wife:

> I have got a delightful plan for the addition at Abb which I think will make it quite complete and furnish me with a handsome library and you with a drawing room and better bedroom with a good bedroom for company etc. It will cost me a little hard work to meet the expense.

By 1823 the new Abbotsford was complete. This time he had created an imposing Baronial mansion with roofs of antique carved oak. With its crow-stepped gables, enclosed forecourt, pepper-pot turrets and castellated tower, Scott had recreated his fictional Tully-Veolan, which he described in the highly successful Waverley novels as boasting 'projections called bartizans, and displayed at each

Here at Abbotsford Scott recreated his very own Tully-Veolan.

The magnificent Baronial style library at Abbotsford.

It was at Abbotsford that Scott wrote *Rob Roy*, *Ivanhoe* and *Waverley*.

frequent angle a small watch tower, rather resembling a pepper box than a Gothic watchtower'.

When finished, Abbotsford's opulence and grand design reflected the writer's enviable status as a respected author and poet, although its critics and detractors believed the money could have been spent more usefully. Situated on the banks of the River Tweed, near Melrose, the Romantic turreted mansion confirmed Scott's financial success at the height of his career and yet, in the end, Scott's elaborate confection, the house that he had dreamed of and longed for and was the affirmation and expression of his success and all that he had achieved, came to represent a financial commitment that, with the benefit of hindsight, he would not have undertaken. By the end of it, he was struggling to settle rising debts in the wake of his extravagant spending and the collapse of his publishing house.

Scott was a partner and chief shareholder in the publishing firm James Ballantyne and when, in 1826, the company became embroiled in the bankruptcy of another publisher, Constable & Co., Scott was found to be liable for the massive debt of £114,000. However, he cannily ensured his creditors could not touch his beloved home by putting it in his son's name – although Scott's strenuous efforts to pay them off undoubtedly shortened his life.

Abbotsford opened to the public in 1833, just a year after Scott's death. But, for much of the twentieth century, Abbotsford – and Scott's own work – was largely bypassed by visitors. His books fell out of fashion as his popularity dwindled and, as the years wore on, he became an increasingly forgotten author.

However, Abbotsford was re-opened by Her Majesty Queen Elizabeth in the early summer of 2013 following a £12 million pro-gramme of extensive improvements, including structural repairs to the crumbling stonework. The new work and the attendant atten-tion has re-awakened interest in both the house, renowned for its Scottish Baronial interior, and its celebrated former occupant.

Inside Abbotsford countless treasures and antiquities vie for attention. Scott's study, completed in 1824, is where he wrote his later novels as well as a nine-volume biography of Bonaparte. The library contains 9,000 rare books and a lock of Bonnie Prince Charlie's hair. A wealth of surviving documentary evidence relating to building work and the decoration of the interiors tells a fascinat-ing story and has proved invaluable during the recent improvement work. Turner spent much of his time sketching at Abbotsford during a stay in 1831 and the artist William Allan created a set of drawings illustrating the layout and furnishing of the main rooms at the time of Scott's death. The pioneering photographer Fox Talbot visited Abbotsford in 1845 and took the first ever photograph of a country house on this scale.

Walter Scott's last descendant to reside at Abbotsford was Dame Jean Maxwell Scott, who died in 2004. Two hundred years after Scott bought Abbotsford and began to shape it as he wished, the house continues to be the subject of improvement and revival as a new chapter in its engrossing story begins.

Referring to Abbotsford, Scott wrote in 1828: 'It is a kind of Conundrum Castle to be sure and I have great pleasure in it for while it pleases a fantastic person in the stile [*sic*] and manner of its architecture and decoration it has all the comforts of a commodious habitation.'

Sir Walter Scott 1771–1832

The ninth of twelve children, Walter Scott was born in Edinburgh where his father was a Writer to the Signet. Scott's childhood was blighted by polio in his right leg, leaving him with a permanent limp. He was sent to his grandfather's farm in Tweeddale to recuperate. It was this period of convalescence that acquainted him with the Romantic landscape of the Border country, its distinctive beauty and its ancient language.

Scott studied at Edinburgh High School and University before starting work in his father's office as a law clerk. He was admitted to the Bar in 1792. By 1799 he was Deputy Sheriff of Selkirk. Deeply influenced by the medieval romance poetry of Italy and France, Scott's attention turned to the colourful Border tales and ballads, which he collected in *The Minstrelsy of the Scottish Border* (1802).

However, his forte lay in the historical novel; his four Waverley stories, *Waverley* (1814), *The Antiquary* (1816), *Old Mortality* (1816) and *The Heart of Midlothian* (1818) became masterpieces and helped establish his reputation as one of Scotland's most influential writers. Many other titles followed and, by the end of his life, his outstanding canon reflected significant historical, literary and antiquarian works written by him or released under his editorship.

He married Margaret Carpenter, originally Charpentier, and the couple had five children. Scott's last years were plagued by ill health and he died at Abbotsford. He is buried in the ruins of nearby Dryburgh Abbey.

DUMFRIES & GALLOWAY

THE ARCHED HOUSE

THE STRONG CALVINIST STREAK in Thomas Carlyle can be traced back to his formative years in south-west Scotland. He was born at the Arched House in Ecclefechan on 4 December 1795 and, until the age of five, was educated at home by his parents, James and Margaret. The eldest of nine children, he learned reading from his mother and was taught arithmetic by his father. The modest, white-washed house of his early childhood was designed and constructed by James Carlyle and the boy's uncle, both of whom were master stonemasons. The Arched House, completed in 1791, takes its name from the large keyed arch that divides the house in two and provides access to a courtyard and garden. Thomas Carlyle was born in the room above the arch, to the right.

The interior of the house is furnished in the style of the period, reflecting domestic life in the latter years of the eighteenth century. Inside is a collection of notable portraits and some of Carlyle's personal belongings and correspondence. The Arched House has been open to the public as a museum since 1883 and has changed little in that time. In contrast to his house in Cheyne Row, Chelsea, The Arched House is small and humble, comprising only three rooms. The kitchen has a large fireplace decorated with stone corbels.

At the time of Thomas Carlyle's birth, Ecclefechan was a typical tight-knit community in Presbyterian Scotland where the pattern of life was routine and predictable. Carlyle began his education at a local primary school where he showed considerable promise, particularly for mathematics. His tutors quickly spotted his aptitude in the classroom, though, typically, Carlyle's propensity for learning was not well received by the school bullies. He was shy and reticent and later found solace in books, studying works by Defoe, Fielding, Congreve and Sterne. In 1806 he attended Annan Academy. His mother argued against it, but Carlyle senior insisted and on 15 May (Whitsunday morning) he and his son walked the six miles to Annan where he was enrolled. While at the academy, Carlyle's attention turned increasingly to modern languages and in later years he taught himself German, Spanish and Italian. However, his interest in books intensified around this time, particularly when he found a well-stocked library within the academy.

Aged fourteen, he prepared to enter university at Edinburgh, to study mathematics and the Classics. Carlyle's path was now destined, yet he never abandoned his roots nor, indeed, his parents, for whom he had the utmost respect and gratitude for their devotion and encouragement during his upbringing. He once described his father as 'among the last of the true men, which Scotland produced or can produce.'

In later life, respected as a champion of morals and social equality, there was always a part of Thomas Carlyle that remained entrenched in his native south-west Scotland, with its simple rituals, age-old traditions and strict religious creed. It did not take much to persuade him to return to the place of his birth: he would regularly travel up to Ecclefechan from London to visit the family tailor when new clothes were required. Fittingly, he insisted that this quiet little town become his final resting-place. His wishes were respected: Thomas Carlyle was buried next to his parents in Ecclefechan churchyard on 5 February 1881. A statue of him was unveiled in the centre of the town almost half a century later, in September 1929. The newly formed BBC broadcast coverage of the event to those with wireless receivers. The National Trust for Scotland acquired the Arched House in 1936.

WALES

SOUTH WALES

THE DYLAN THOMAS BIRTHPLACE MUSEUM

THROUGHOUT HIS SHORT BUT eventful life, Dylan Thomas's mind and imagination never strayed far from the city of his birth or the mystical land that influenced his talent and his extraordinary gift for words. Wherever he went in the world, whether it be drinking and roistering in the pubs of London or entertaining audiences with poetry recitals in the United States (by then firmly on the path to self-destruction), there was a part of him that was forever Swansea, the 'ugly, lovely town' of his formative years.

Time and again Thomas would return to his native Wales and time and again his mind would hark back to the idyllic childhood he had spent in the Uplands region of the city, playing in Cwmdonkin Park just across the way from the family home, and sitting in his tiny bedroom, writing poetry and staring out of the window at the solid, plain wall of the house next door. Much of his published work was conceived in this room. According to Jon Tregenna, the writer and curator of the Boat House at Laugharne: 'The whole place creeks of him; it's like a thousand ghosts.'

I have a particular affection for the house in Cwmdonkin Drive, which today can be rented for self-catering breaks and holidays. It was here, by the kindness of the owners, that I stayed overnight, actually sleeping in Thomas's old bedroom, while researching the life and work of the great poet. Few literary shrines offer such an experience.

Thomas was born at 5 Cwmdonkin Drive, which he described as 'a provincial villa ... a small, not very well painted gateless house ... very nice, very respective'. Thomas's family was middle-class and the four-bedroom, semi-detached house in this respectable,

During his childhood Dylan Thomas could often be found at the window of his parents' bedroom in Cwmdonkin Drive, gazing over the city's roof tops to the ships in Swansea Bay.

hilly district of Swansea was new when his parents and older sister, Nancy, moved there in 1914 shortly before he was born.

Having gained a first-class honours degree in English literature, Thomas's father, a Carmarthenshire man, believed he might become a university lecturer or professor. However, his true ambition was never realized and he ended up teaching English at Swansea Grammar School, which was attended by the young Thomas and in more recent years, Geoff Haden, who, with his wife Anne, bought 5 Cwmdonkin Drive in 2008, restoring it authentically to the style of the early twentieth century when the Thomas family lived there.

A look at the study puts Dylan Thomas's love of words into context. In this room, while only a small child aged just four, Dylan was taught by his scholarly, academically unfulfilled father and encouraged by him to read Shakespeare and the Classics. Thomas senior even read the work of the Bard aloud in order to help his young son gain an ear for the sound of words and language. On the first floor the boy would stare out of the window of his parents' bedroom at the back of the house, gazing out at the ships and the sweep of Swansea Bay – 'the long and splendid curving shore'. The view enthralled him.

232

Among the artefacts pointing to the early life of the poet genius is a copy of *Boys Own*, dated November 1923. Included in the magazine is 'His Requiem', a poem composed by Lillian Gard, but plagiarized by Thomas, then aged twelve or thirteen, who then sent it to the *Western Mail*, Wales's own national newspaper, under his own name. Thomas, whose ambition was to be as good a poet as Keats, if not better, was paid for the piece, although the fee, a postal order, was never cashed. Instead, it was framed and hung in the house as a proud reminder of the boy's successful early foray into publishing. The truth eventually came to light almost fifty years later, but by then Dylan Thomas was long dead, although his fame and reputation are everlasting.

While growing up in Swansea, Thomas's favourite destination was Cwmdonkin Park, the childhood haunt of many of his friends and associates during those early years. The park, consisting of trees, ponds and neat lawns, was the perfect playground and, for Thomas, in particular, it was a magical place that fired his imagination. 'That Cwmdonkin Park was a world within the world of the sea town', he wrote. 'We would explore it, armed and desperate, from end to end.'

Dylan Thomas moved to London in 1934 but returned to Cwmdonkin Drive on occasion before his parents let the villa and moved to a smaller house close to the sea at nearby Bishopston in 1937.

THE BOAT HOUSE

DYLAN THOMAS MAY HAVE been a struggling poet for much of his life, but he found riches of a very different kind when he and his wife Caitlin moved to the Boat House at Laugharne, forty miles west of Swansea, in the spring of 1949. Few writers have been fortunate enough to acquire a home perched, quite literally, on the water's edge, with unrivalled views across a beautiful expansive estuary. Apart from the plaintive cries of the seabirds and the water lapping gently against the shore, there are no sounds, nothing to disturb the overwhelming tranquillity of the place. The Boat House's glorious setting on the Taf estuary remains exactly as it was when Thomas lived and worked there, exposed to the elements but mercifully overlooked by the rest of the world.

The poet fell in love with Laugharne the moment he saw what he called 'the strangest town in Wales'. Four years later he would be married and living in the Carmarthenshire town, although the move to the Boat House came later. 'I wish I could describe what I am looking on,' he told Pamela Hansford Johnson, a poet and former girlfriend. His words paint a vivid picture of the town and its remote waterside setting: 'the miles and miles of mud and grey sand ... the mean-souled cries of the gulls and herons'.

It was Thomas's old friend and patron Margaret Taylor, wife of the historian A.J.P. Taylor, who found him the perfect retreat. She paid £3,000 for a lease on the Boat House, which the poet and his wife had always viewed as the house of their dreams. Taylor even managed to find a property to rent in the centre of Laugharne for Thomas's parents.

Originally the site of a coal-yard where cargo boats would

The Boat House at Laugharne was Dylan Thomas's perfect Welsh retreat and where he spent his final years.

berth, the Boat House was acquired by a Worcestershire doctor in the early years of the twentieth century for use as a holiday home. However, it was a different story by the time the Thomas family moved in. The house was basic and rudimentary, there was no running water or electricity and the red sandstone cliff looming directly above the property, compounded by water lapping constantly against the lower walls at high tide, created a damp, uninviting environment. Yet the house had to fulfil the needs of a growing family: the Thomas's had two children with a third expected. Taylor soon installed mains services while Caitlin set about transforming the interior. Nevertheless, life was far from easy; the erratic nature of Thomas's work meant that money was tight and the family lived a precarious, hand-to-mouth existence.

A flight of steps rose above the roofline of the house to a path leading into Laugharne. The town, renowned for its romantic ruined castle and striking Norman church, lies a stone's throw from the

On a bluff above the Boat House stands the shed in which Dylan Thomas worked somewhat erratic hours. It is known that after drinking at nearby Brown's Hotel, he would return to this shed and invariably sleep for several hours.

Boat House. A matter of yards from the top of the steps is a small wooden shed, built in 1925, where the doctor who resided at the house kept his Wolsey. This simple building, with its breathtaking view of the estuary, was where Dylan Thomas spent his working hours.

The shed, his eyrie, his 'water and tree room on the cliff', became a place of cosy familiarity. Thomas covered the walls with pictures and there were also photographs of his favourite writers, including one of Edith Sitwell. The shed is rarely open to visitors, but a glance through the window reveals a typical writer's study, cluttered and untidy and strewn with books, cigarette packets and discarded notes. The room may have been chaotic, but the view inspired many of Thomas's poems. Here he would observe the ritualistic practices of the local birdlife, the eternal cycle of the tide and the variable, often dramatic, weather conditions of the estuary.

Thomas had his own fairly predictable routine at the Boat House. He would read in the morning before sauntering along the well-worn path into Laugharne. There he would visit his parents and complete *The Times* crossword with his father. About noon he would cross the road to Brown's Hotel, his favourite hostelry, for a pint or two and a chat with the locals. Although apparently Thomas's mother always insisted to others that her son did not drink, she made sure he knew she was aware of his adventures at Brown's. 'Now, don't think I'm interfering, dear, I just happened to be looking out of the window as you fell down Brown's steps', she would say to him.

Drunk or sober, Thomas would leave the bar about two o'clock and return to the shed. During the winter months an anthracite stove gradually took the chill off his little work-room while he was out. He would remain in the shed until early evening and then adjourn next door to the Boat House. After a hot bath, during which he would sit eating sweets or pickled onions, he would settle down to a family meal. However, the thought of a pint and a little socializing in the friendly surroundings of a familiar bar would draw him back to Brown's once more.

The Boat House is owned today by the local corporation and leased to Carmarthenshire County Council. Dylan Thomas's former home draws many visitors throughout the year, some of whom make their way to Brown's Hotel in Laugharne as part of the pilgrimage, perhaps to drink a toast to the great man and picture him in full flow at the bar. I finished my tour of the town with a visit to the church where a simple cross marks Thomas's grave. A bouquet of flowers left by a fan brightened the scene, but it was the simple inscription on the card that said so much more about the man, his supreme talent and his extraordinary legacy. 'Thank you for the words, Dylan.'

Dylan Thomas 1914–53

Thomas recalled his first school in Swansea as 'firm and kind and smelling of galoshes'. He could never be described as a model pupil and his apparent lack of respect for authority was also evident when he progressed to Swansea Grammar School. He was regarded as a most unorthodox schoolboy and a highly individual, non-conformist figure in the classroom. Education and learning didn't interest him. He was far happier exploring his surroundings and observing the plain, the commonplace and the ordinary. It proved to be fertile ground.

As his father taught at the same school, Thomas enjoyed a certain freedom within its boundaries, escaping punishment for truancy and general misbehaviour. Leaving school early one day, he was confronted by the headmaster who demanded to know where the boy was going. 'Home to my poetry,' replied Thomas. 'Well, don't get caught then,' replied the headmaster. However, Thomas's reputation improved when he became editor of the school magazine.

Thomas left school in 1931 aged sixteen and began work as a journalist on the *South Wales Evening Post*. He wasn't an especially good or talented reporter and was later sacked. By now the bohemian culture of Swansea had captured his heart and imagination and he spent much of the inter-war years socializing in the city of his birth.

With his wild, passionate nature and abiding love of language, Dylan Thomas embodies so many of his country's renowned characteristics, and he is still seen as a key influence in the long cultural history of Wales. Thomas's first volume of verse, *18 Poems*, appeared in 1934, the year he moved to London. Once there, he soon became an integral part of the hard-drinking Grub Street culture of journalism that prevailed at the time. Thomas also established himself as a radio broadcaster and a popular entertainer, his character and love of words ideally suited to this media. In 1937 he married Caitlin Macnamara, a model who sat for Augustus John.

From 1944 he worked spasmodically on a short play, *Quite Early One Morning*. Created for radio and describing an early morning coastal walk, the piece is thought to have inspired Thomas's 'play for voices', with which he remains most closely associated. In effect, it is his epitaph. Written while Thomas was living at the Boat House, *Under Milk Wood* (1954) was also adapted as a stage play and later filmed with his old friend Richard Burton playing the part of the narrator.

Dylan Thomas, the rolling Welsh boyo, forever ebullient, turbulent and untamed, died in New York from excessive alcohol abuse while on a lecture tour of the United States of America. He was thirty-nine. He is remembered as a genius whose love of words earned him international respect and admiration. However, he could be contrary and mercurial about his work. He once said: 'Poetry is not the most important thing in life ... I'd much rather lie in a hot bath, reading Agatha Christie and sucking sweets.'

NORTH WALES

PLAS NEWYDD

SEEN WITHIN THE CONTEXT of polite Georgian society, it must have been an extraordinary spectacle. On 30 March 1778, two aristocratic Irish spinsters, dressed as men and armed with pistols, rode through the night to catch the ferry at Waterford, on the south-eastern coast of Ireland. They were Lady Eleanor Butler, the elder of the two, and Sarah Ponsonby. Sarah was carrying her dog, Frisk. The ferry did not sail that night and their families eventually caught up with them just outside the port. Undaunted, the couple made plans yet again to go away together. On this occasion, however, it was with the full permission of their relatives. They were granted an annual allowance of £280.

Accompanied by their devoted housemaid, Mary Carryll, they toured North Wales, their travels taking them to Llangollen, then one of the key staging posts between England and Ireland. The two women settled here in 1780, making their home at Plas Newydd, Denbighshire, a rented stone cottage standing in twelve acres of formal garden just outside the town. It was where they remained for the rest of their lives – almost fifty years – and in time their names and reputations were so closely associated with this part of the country that they became known as the 'Ladies of Llangollen'.

Butler and Ponsonby had been friends for almost ten years by the time they fled their homes that early spring night. They lived near one another in Ireland and enjoyed a close friendship, though initially the age gap between them provoked some surprise – Ponsonby being a schoolgirl of thirteen when they met and Butler a woman in her late twenties. At Plas Newydd they enjoyed shared interests, including writing, reading and gardening. The two women also carried out various improvements to the cottage. Over the years, they extended and embellished it, incorporating striking Gothic windows with stained-glass panels. Elaborately carved oak also featured heavily in the design work.

Though their relationship was close – they shared a bed and referred to each other as 'my beloved' and 'my better half' – there is no evidence it was sexual. True, they breached the bounds of convention of the time, but they can also be seen as two eccentric women who were determined to kick over the traces, defy the protocol and formality of the period, and live as they chose in 'delicious retirement'. Not surprisingly, however, their actions sparked outrage and indignation within their social circle and among their own class. They became the talk of London and Dublin coffee shops. Indeed, the events leading to their eventual, settled existence at Plas Newydd were so melodramatic and richly drawn, it was as if they belonged among the pages of an historical novel.

In today's more enlightened world, their decision to set up home together would be seen as commonplace. In the final years of the eighteenth century, however, two women living together would have been viewed with fear and suspicion. All manner of rumour began to circulate both locally and in the wider world. Even in later years they were believed to be spies, suffragettes or men dressed as women.

Others were intrigued by, or even envious of, their apparently blissful domestic arrangements while, inevitably, there were those who were curious as to the true nature of their ambiguous relationship. None of it really mattered to Butler and Ponsonby. They had achieved their aim to live together in joyous union.

In time their fame and reputation spread and several years after the move to North Wales, they received a letter from Queen Charlotte, who wished to learn more about their cottage and garden. She was so enamoured of the two devoted friends, she persuaded her husband, George III, to grant them a pension. Butler and Ponsonby rapidly became celebrities of their day and counted among their many friends the Duke of Wellington. William Wordsworth and Robert Southey were admirers too, composing poems upon them while at Plas Newydd, though Wordsworth's description of their home as 'a low-roofed cot' was not well received. Sir Walter Scott came to Llangollen with the Scottish biographer and novelist John Lockhart. Byron and Shelley were equally impressed by the achievements of the two women, and Lady Caroline Lamb, who conducted a passionate affair with Byron and was a distant relative of Ponsonby, also visited.

Butler and Ponsonby were not published writers themselves and therefore to entertain the likes of Wordsworth, Southey and Scott at home would have been an experience to treasure. How the house must have echoed to the sound of stimulating conversation and eloquent prose! Butler kept a diary and the two women studied literature and learned languages, but they could never have imagined while growing up in Ireland and during those early years at Plas Newydd that they would eventually become acquainted with some of Britain's leading poets and writers. It is not inconceivable that, to a degree, these distinguished literary figures were themselves inspired by the 'Ladies of Llangollen'.

However, life at Plas Newydd was not perfect. Butler and Ponsonby had to endure jealousies, financial difficulties and unwelcome newspaper reports concerning their private life. Despite these problems, they managed to purchase the cottage, thus guaranteeing continuity at their secluded Welsh retreat. Both women died there and are buried beneath a neo-Gothic tombstone in Llangollen churchyard. Following their deaths, General John Yorke bought Plas Newydd, re-designing the front of the house and introducing a black and white, half-timbered façade. Inside is the Oak Room where Butler and Ponsonby's initials can be seen carved into the over-mantle. Llangollen Urban District Council acquired the house in 1932 and retained many of the Gothic features introduced by Butler and Ponsonby. Plas Newydd remains a museum, managed by Denbighshire County Council.

Eleanor Butler 1739–1829

The youngest daughter of Walter Butler, the *de jure* Earl of Ormond of Kilkenny Castle, Eleanor Butler was born not in Ireland, but at Cambrai, France. Considered an upper-class Catholic, she was educated abroad before living at Kilkenny Castle for twelve years. Kilkenny was the principal Irish home of the influential Butler family for almost 600 years. Regarded among the family to be unfeminine and satirical, it was thought unlikely that Butler would marry.

Sarah Ponsonby 1755–1831

The orphaned daughter of Chambre Brabazon Ponsonby, a cousin of the Earl of Bessborough, Sarah Ponsonby was educated at Kilkenny. After completing her education, she went to live with distant relatives at nearby Woodstock House, where she experienced the unwelcome attentions of her middle-aged guardian. Sarah Ponsonby was described as shy and bookish by nature.

CAE'R GORS

THE SHORT-STORY WRITER AND novelist Kate Roberts is often referred to as the 'Queen of our literature.' Coming from a poor, slate-quarrying family from Caernarfonshire, it was perhaps inevitable that she would draw on the hardship and challenges of such an existence as background material for her work. It proved to be fertile ground. In her memoirs, published in 1960, she wrote: 'The people of my time were people fighting against poverty...we never saw wealth, but we had a wealth that nobody could take away from us, the wealth of language and culture.' Her childhood home was Cae'r Gors, a modest, Grade II* listed cottage and smallholding in the village of Rhosgadfan, near Caernarfon. Roberts lived there between the ages of four and eighteen.

Years later, in the mid-1960s, she bought the stone-built, quarryman's dwelling, by then a roofless ruin, and gave it to the nation. However, it was forty years before funding allowed restoration work to go ahead. Today, the cottage and surrounding buildings form a heritage and community centre celebrating the life of Kate Roberts and her family. The interior reflects the late Victorian era and the early years of the twentieth century, the period during which Roberts lived at Cae'r Gors. The name is Welsh for 'marsh field'.

For the Roberts family, the daily routine at the cottage was simple and predictable. Typically, the men in these communities worked in the quarries, while the women ran the house and toiled on the land. As a child, Roberts would go out early in the morning to gather heather and gorse for the fire and on her return she would cook porridge. Adjacent to the dwelling are a few acres where the family kept pigs, sheep and cows. The hillsides around Rhosgadfan are littered with similar buildings, though many have been converted and modernized over the years.

In 1972 Roberts drew a sketch plan of Cae'r Gors, which she enclosed with a letter sent to the offices of the Royal Commission on Ancient and Historical Monuments Wales, describing her home. The plan provided a strong indication of the layout during her formative years at the cottage. The kitchen was open to the roof and heated by a large chimney; there was no staircase; and a ladder provided access to the loft over the front parlour/bedroom.

Roberts had left Rhosgadfan by the time she began writing, though as a child growing up in the village her imagination would have been captured by the culture and mythology of her native Wales, following in the tradition of the great literary figures of her own generation and those preceding. However, it was the death in 1917 of her youngest brother, David, following injuries received in battle that impelled her to write. His needless loss at such an early age was a bitter blow and she knew she had to find a way to come to terms with his death and the circumstances surrounding it. 'I had to start writing or suffocate,' she wrote.

Various volumes of short stories followed, then a novel, *Feet in Chains*, published in 1936, which took as its main theme the austerity and the relentless struggle against poverty Roberts had witnessed while growing up in rural Wales. The harsh conditions and social inequality of the period represent the narrative running through her work. Perhaps her most successful book is *Tea in the Heather* (1959), a brilliant evocation, in the form of a series of stories, of traditional family life among the slate quarries and smallholdings Roberts knew so well.

> ## Kate Roberts 1891–1985
>
> One of the foremost Welsh-language writers of the twentieth century and a prominent Welsh nationalist, Catherine (Kate) Roberts was the eldest of four children. She attended the University College of North Wales at Bangor, where she graduated in Welsh and gained her teaching certificate. Roberts taught at several schools in South Wales before she married Morris Williams, a printer, in 1928. They met through the newly established Welsh Nationalist Party. In 1935 the couple acquired Gwasg Gee (the Gee Press), a printing and publishing house in Denbigh.
>
> Together, Roberts and Williams published books and leaflets and a significant volume of material promoting the theme of Welsh language. Williams died in 1946 and Roberts single-handedly ran the business for the next ten years. She remained in Denbigh after her retirement. The role of women in society is one of the major themes of her work and Roberts is also acknowledged as pioneering the modern version of the short story in Welsh. Her work has been translated into English, French and German. She lived to advanced old age and died aged 94. Kate Roberts is buried at Denbigh.

YR YSGWRN

DEEP IN THE ROLLING countryside of Snowdonia lies Yr Ysgwrn, a small farm, remote and barely visible at the end of a track outside the village of Trawsfynydd. From it, on a good day, the outline of Mount Snowdon is visible and all around are lush green hills and glimpses of distant peaks. From the track leading to Yr Ysgwrn, the place looks unremarkable; a typical, traditional Welsh farmstead not unlike hundreds of other rural settlements in this part of North Wales. However, there is much that sets it apart from the other farms in the area. Entering the mid-nineteenth-century stone farmhouse, you sense a world and a way of life that have long since vanished into memory. It is as if time has stood still. Yr Ysgwrn is an extraordinary place by any standards, stunning in its simplicity and virtually unchanged or untouched by the passing of the years for a century.

Yr Ysgwrn was the home of Ellis Humphrey Evans, who, as Hedd Wyn (a bardic name meaning 'blessed peace'), became one

SNPA AND THE YR YSGWRN FAMILY

Yr Ysgwrn, the former home of the Welsh-language poet, Ellis Evans.

of the country's most respected and revered Welsh-language poets. Evans grew up at the farm, which lay at the heart of a region steeped in the tradition and culture of Wales and in the language of Welsh poetry. In many ways, he was a typical Welshman – deeply patriotic and immensely proud of his country's cultural heritage. However, he also came to symbolize a lost generation and the utter pointlessness and futility of a war that saw the slaughter of thousands of his countrymen. Evans died of injuries sustained during the battle for Pilckem Ridge in Flanders on 31 July 1917. He was only thirty years old.

After only six years of formal education, Ellis Evans began work at Yr Ysgwrn. He was twelve. He might not have taken readily to farming, but he knew every inch of this wild Welsh landscape. It was in his soul and where he belonged. It was this affinity with his surroundings, the character and spirit of North Wales and the vagaries of the elements that inspired his writing, in which there is a powerful sense of people and place. 'Give my regards to the wind and the rain of Trawsfynydd,' he wrote in a letter to a villager while working briefly at a colliery in South Wales.

Evans became acquainted with the work of the leading Romantic poets and would often sit for hours by the fire in the *cegin* (kitchen) at Yr Ysgwrn, staying up long into the night, reading poetry and working on his own compositions. His sister Maggie, rising early the following morning to light the fire, would find him fast asleep, slumped over a scattered sheaf of notes. She would immediately tidy the papers and insist he go to bed.

His dedication paid off. From the age of nineteen Evans began winning prizes at local eisteddfods. Early in 1917, with war raging in Europe, he enlisted with the 15th battalion of the Royal Welsh Fusiliers at Blaenau Ffestiniog. He left for Flanders in June. While enlisted, Private Evans returned to Yr Ysgwrn for two weeks' leave. During this time he sat down at the table in the *cegin* and wrote a poem entitled *Yr arwr* (The Hero). The weather was wet and dismal, and he chose to stay for a further seven days. Though the exact circumstances of his leave and subsequent return to the Western Front are unclear, it has been claimed he was deemed a deserter and arrested by military police while working on the farm. In the confusion that would have ensued, he forgot the poem and wrote a second copy from memory during the return journey.

On reaching the Front, Evans submitted the poem to the eisteddfod office by post, using the pseudonym 'Fleur-de-lis'. In September, 'The Hero' was awarded the prestigious chair at the national

Most of the bardic chairs arrived at nearby Trawsfynydd by train. Several may have been carried to Yr Ysgwrn on foot.

eisteddfod held that year in Birkenhead. David Lloyd George was present and made a speech calling for victory against Germany no matter what the cost. The winner of the principal literary prize that year was announced, but the recipient was absent. Evans had been killed in battle just six weeks before. As a mark of respect, the chair was draped in black. Members of the audience were visibly upset and an overwhelming sense of loss pervaded the room.

The Evans family received £10 in prize money and a medal for freedom and honour issued by the War Office in recognition of his military service and ultimate sacrifice. The chair, decorated with a Celtic cross, a two-headed serpent and a symbol of familial pattern and order – among other features – was brought from Birkenhead to Yr Ysgwrn by train and horse and cart. The bardic chairs of six eisteddfodau remain at the farm, proudly displayed in the small front parlour and watched over by the poet himself, his striking features visible in several stark photographs hanging on the walls.

The *cegin*, the larger of the two rooms on view, is the heart of the house and has not altered substantially since Evans spent his formative years here. The fields in which he toiled as a youth can be seen from the window and the glow of the fire

The *cegin* at Yr Ysgwrn has changed little since Ellis Evans lived at the farm.

attempts to banish the shadows of the room in the gathering gloom of a winter's afternoon. On display are a traditional Welsh dresser with willow pattern plates, a grandfather clock and a piano, moved here from the parlour many years ago to make room for the bardic chairs.

In 2012 Snowdonia National Park was awarded a grant to preserve Yr Ysgwrn for future generations. Little will change at the Grade II* listed house in the years ahead, and the decision to maintain Yr Ysgwrn honours a pledge made by Mary Evans, Ellis's mother, to 'keep the door open' to visitors from all corners of the world seeking to visit the modest home of a cherished poet whose name is not forgotten.

I sang to the long hope of my life
And the magic of the inspiration of youth;
The passion of the wind and the scent
Of the lighting of the path
Ahead were in my poem.

My muse was a deep cry
And all the ages to come will hear it
And my rewards were grievous violence;
And a world that is
One long bare winter without respite.

From *The Hero*

Ellis Evans 1887–1917

The eldest of eleven children and the son of a hill farmer, Ellis Humphrey Evans was born at Pen-lan in the village of Trawsfynydd, about one mile from Yr Ysgwrn. In addition to agricultural labouring, he worked as a shepherd at the farm.

Evans was a shy man, with a mischievous sense of humour. He was also a committed socialist and a Christian. Images of war influenced his prose and his impressions and observations of daily life at the Front are evident, even in correspondence. In a letter to a friend, he wrote: 'Heavy weather, heavy soul, heavy heart. That is an unforgettable Trinity isn't it? I never saw a land more beautiful in spite of the curse that has landed upon it.' Following his death, a collection of his poems was published under the title *Cerddi'r bugail* ('Poems of the Shepherd'). Ellis Evans was buried in Artillery Wood Cemetery near Boezinge in Belgium.

WRITERS' RETREATS

OTHER PLACES OF INTEREST

To complement the houses described earlier in this book, this section is devoted to a small selection of varied buildings and structures, all of which have literary associations and have some, if limited, access to the public.

ENGLAND

THE ROALD DAHL MUSEUM & STORY CENTRE

THE WRITER ROALD DAHL (1916–90) considered his writing hut a vital element of his daily routine. He would go there every morning about ten and begin by sharpening his pencils, which he kept in a toby jug. After about two hours devoted to writing, the pencils would need sharpening again. Around the middle of the day he would enjoy a light lunch, followed by a nap and a flutter on the horses before returning to the hut where he would write for a further two hours.

The writing hut was not particularly well lit and in the winter it would be filled with the pungent smell of a paraffin heater. A single-bar electric heater hung from the ceiling and Dahl would sit with a rug draped over him and his legs encased in a sleeping bag. Many years after Dahl's death a decision was taken on the future of the hut. To preserve it in situ wasn't viable; instead it was moved to

a permanent site within the Roald Dahl Museum and Story Centre, where it can now be seen.

HENRY WILLIAMSON'S WRITING HUT

Given Grade II-listed status by English heritage, the hut was built in 1929 by Henry Williamson (1895–1977), two years after the publication of *Tarka the Otter*, for which he won the Hawthornden Prize for Literature. The prize money paid for his spartan, elm-board retreat, which can be found on a hill above the village of the North Devon coastal village of Georgeham. Inside, Williamson's boots can be seen, along with his plaid jacket and spectacles.

Williamson would often spend up to fifteen hours a day in the hut, and it was here he wrote his long series *A Chronicle of Ancient Sunlight* (1951–69).

SCOTLAND

BARNHILL

THE WRITER WILL SELF has described the walk to Barnhill on the remote island of Jura as 'one of the most profound, beautiful and moving journeys anyone can take on this earth.' Five miles off the west coast of Scotland, the island is where George Orwell – the pseudonym of Eric Arthur Blair (1903–50) – sought solitude to write his classic novel *Nineteen Eighty-Four*. He stayed at Barnhill, an isolated house at the northern end of Jura, where the writer spent much of the last three years of his life. He finished the novel in 1948.

Today, Barnhill is let as self-catering accommodation and is surely one of the loneliest holiday retreats in Britain. There is an ancient diesel generator for electric light and a small, gas-powered fridge.

WHALSAY

WHALSAY IS THE SIXTH largest of the Shetland Islands. During the 1930s and early 1940s, the Scottish poet Hugh MacDiarmid – pseudonym of Christopher Murray Grieve (1892–1978) – lived here and was inspired by its beauty and solitude to create some of his finest work. More than half his output was written on Whalsay and while on the island he became increasingly preoccupied with geology and the landscape – themes that are reflected in his writing.

MacDiarmid's home at Sudheim is now a camping böd – modest self-catering accommodation in traditional Shetland buildings.

WALES

SNOWDON LODGE

RUN TODAY AS A youth hostel, this four-bedroom Grade II Victorian villa on the edge of the Llŷn Peninsula was built in 1880, eight years before the birth of T.E. Lawrence (1888–1935) who, it is claimed, was delivered in one of the first-floor front bedrooms. Lawrence was born illegitimate; his father, Thomas Chapman, seventh Baron of Westmeath, left his wife and set up home with Sarah Junner, a governess. They lived together as a family, leaving the house in Tremadog after little more than a year. T.E. Lawrence was not Welsh, but the place of his birth earned him the right to be called 'an honorary Welshman'.

SELECT BIBLIOGRAPHY

Ackroyd, P., *Shakespeare: The Biography* (Chatto & Windus, 2005)

Barker, J., *The Brontës: A Life in Letters* (Viking, 1997)

Beer, A., *Milton: Pamphleteer and Patriot* (Bloomsbury, 2008)

Byrne, P., *Mad World: Evelyn Waugh and the Secrets of Brideshead* (HarperPress, 2009)

Chaney, L., *Hide-and-Seek with Angels: The Life of J.M. Barrie* (Arrow Books, 2006)

Davies, H., *William Wordsworth: A Biography* (Sutton Publishing, 1997)

Dennison, M., *Behind the Mask: the Life of Vita Sackville-West* (Harper-Collins, 2014)

Dunn, J., *Daphne du Maurier and Her Sisters: The Hidden Lives of Piffy, Bird and Bing* (HarperPress, 2013)

Fowler-Wright, S., *The Life of Sir Walter Scott* (Borgo Press, 2012)

Hardyment, C., *Literary Trails: Writers in their Landscapes* (Abrams, 2000)

Hardyment, C., *Writing Britain: Wastelands to Wonderlands* (British Library, 2012)

Harris, A., *Virginia Woolf* (Thames & Hudson, 2011)

Hastings, S., *Evelyn Waugh: A Biography* (Sinclair Stevenson, 1994)

Heffer, S., *Moral Desperado: A Life of Thomas Carlyle* (Weidenfeld & Nicolson, 1995)

Hillier, B., *Betjeman: The Bonus of Laughter* (John Murray, 2004)

Hird, D. & E. Young, *Disraeli: or the Two Lives* (Weidenfeld & Nicolson, 2013)

Hughes, K., *George Eliot: The Last Victorian* (Fourth Estate, 1998)

Janes, H., *The Three Lives of Dylan Thomas* (The Robson Press, 2014)

Jenkins, S., *England's Thousand Best Houses* (Allen Lane, 2003)

Kaplan, F., *Henry James: The Imagination of Genius* (John Hopkins University Press, 1999)

Korda, M., *Hero: The Life and Legend of Lawrence of Arabia* (Aurum Press, 2012)

Lear, L., *Beatrix Potter: The Extraordinary Life of a Victorian Genius* (Penguin, 2008)

Lee, H., *Virginia Woolf* (Vintage, 1997)

Lycett, A., *Conan Doyle: The Man who Created Sherlock Holmes* (Weidenfeld & Nicolson, 2007)

Lycett, A., *Dylan Thomas: A New Life* (Weidenfeld & Nicolson, 2004)

Lycett Green, C., *The Dangerous Edge of Things* (Doubleday, 2005)

MacCarthy, F., *Byron: Life and Legend* (Faber & Faber, 2002)

Macaskill, H., *Daphne du Maurier at Home* (Frances Lincoln, 2013)

McDowell, M., *Beatrix Potter's Gardening Life* (Timber Press, 2013)

McGrath, A., *C.S. Lewis: A Life* (Hodder & Stoughton, 2013)

McIntyre, I., *Robert Burns: A Life* (Constable, 2009)

Martin, P., *Samuel Johnson: A Biography* (Weidenfeld & Nicolson, 2008)

Marsh, K. (edited by), *Writers and their Houses* (Hamish Hamilton, 1993)

Motion, A., *Keats* (Faber & Faber, 2005)

Mulvagh, J., *Madresfield: The Real Brideshead* (Doubleday, 2008)

Nokes, D., *Samuel Johnson* (Faber & Faber, 2009)

Reef, C., *The Brontë Sisters: The Brief Lives of Charlotte, Emily and Anne* (Houghton Mifflin, 2012)

Sackville-West, V. & S. Raven, *Vita Sackville-West's Sissinghurst* (Virago, 2014)

Shelston, A., *Brief Lives: Elizabeth Gaskell* (Hesperus Press, 2010)

Slater, M., *Charles Dickens* (Yale, 2009)

Struthers, J. & C. Coe, *Literary Britain and Ireland* (New Holland, 2005)

Thompson, L., *Agatha Christie: An English Mystery* (Headline Review, 2007)

Tomalin, C., *Jane Austen – A Life* (Penguin, 2012)

Tomalin, C., *Charles Dickens – A Life* (Viking, 2011)

Tomalin, C., *Thomas Hardy: The Time-Torn Man* (Viking, 2006)

Uglow, J., *Elizabeth Gaskell: A Habit of Stories* (Faber & Faber, 1999)

Wilson, A. N., *C.S. Lewis: A Biography* (William Collins Sons & Co Ltd, 1990)

Worthen, J., *D.H. Lawrence: The Life of an Outsider* (Allen Lane, 2005)

PICTURE CREDITS

All images by the author unless specified below. Page numbers are given in bold.

(233) John Levin [CC by 2.0 (http://creativecommons.org/licenses/by-sa/2.0/legalcode)]

(234) Carmarthenshire County Council

(245, 246 & 247) Snowdonia National Park Authority (SNPA) and the Ysgwrn family

(250) The Roald Dahl Museum and Story Centre

INDEX

Images are shown in *italics*